The processes outlined in Five Easy Steps *became a critical component of our district's Mathematics Strategic Plan beginning in 1998.* Five Easy Steps to a Balanced Math Program *provided practical suggestions to assist our teachers with the implementation of the district's mathematics program, [including] its required instructional components. While the Mathematics Strategic Plan serves as an umbrella for the district's efforts,* Five Easy Steps to a Balanced Math Program *provided clarity of purpose and a systemic way of maintaining the focus.*

As a result, student achievement has steadily increased while the achievement gap has narrowed. Our work with Five Easy Steps to a Balanced Math Program *has been one of the factors responsible for these improved results.*

> Denise M. Walston
> Senior Coordinator—Mathematics
> (K–12)
> Norfolk Public Schools
> Norfolk, VA

Five Easy Steps *has strengthened our traditional math curriculum by providing our staff with solid foundation in research-based math instruction. The implementation process focused on the consistency of strategies across the grades and gave the teachers a common language for discussing Mental Math, Math Review, concept development, and problem solving. After three years of implementation, our district continues to show impressive gains on the state assessments for all the NCLB subgroups.*

> Susan Schwicardi, Ed.D.
> Assistant Superintendent for
> Curriculum and Instruction
> District 45
> Villa Park, IL

Excellent program! I have enjoyed following the Five Easy Steps *model, particularly the warm-ups. I use them almost daily at the beginning of class, revisiting skills on a regular basis. This year I have begun to incorporate the weekly quiz component, and am finding it a valuable tool to quickly assess my students on new material, and the results I use to help plan the next week's agenda.*

Angie Brown
Teacher
Fall Creek Valley Middle School
Indianapolis, IN

Our use of the Five Easy Steps to a Balanced Math Program *framework has made an astounding difference in our students' ability to reason, think, and be successful in math! The framework provides for a variety of learning experiences that have helped our teachers learn how to differentiate mathematics learning for our students and help them to develop conceptual understanding of math topics. The student success is apparent in their daily classroom activities and is being transferred to our statewide testing results. We love it!*

Jodi Peyton
Digital Age Literacy Coach
Metropolitan School District
of Lawrence Township
Indianapolis, IN

Five Easy Steps to a Balanced Math Program for Secondary Grades

Larry Ainsworth

Jan Christinson

A L P
**Advanced
Learning
Press**

Advanced Learning Press

317 Inverness Way South, Suite 150
Englewood, CO 80112
Phone (800) 844-6599 or (303) 504-9312 ● Fax (303) 504-9417
www.AdvancedLearningPress.com

Advanced Learning Press also publishes books in a variety of electronic formats.
Some content that appears in print may not be available in electronic books.

Library of Congress Cataloging-in-Publication Data

Ainsworth, Larry.
    Five easy steps to a balanced math program for secondary grades : middle school & high school /
Larry Ainsworth, Jan Christinson.
        p.   cm.
Includes bibliographical references and index.
    ISBN-13: 978-1-933196-24-4
    ISBN-10: 1-933196-24-6
    1. Mathematics — Study and teaching (Middle school)—United States.   2. Mathematics —
Study and teaching (Secondary)—United States.   I. Christinson, Jan.   II. Title.
    QA13.A42   2006
    372.7—dc22   2006042758

Printed in the United States of America

10 09 08 07 06   01 02 03 04 05 06 07 08 09

Contents

Contents

Contents

Contents

Contents

Contents

Acknowledgments

Since the initial publication of *Five Easy Steps to a Balanced Math Program* in 2000, math educators and leaders nationwide have found the framework of these five steps to be effective for designing and delivering the key components of a comprehensive math program. It was this success that led to our decision to write three separate books—one each for the primary, upper elementary, and secondary grades—rather than one second edition attempting to address kindergarten through high school grades. We wish to acknowledge and thank our publisher, Anne Fenske of Advanced Learning Press, for her diligent support of and commitment to this project. We also wish to extend our special thanks to George Foster of Foster Covers, Brooke Graves of Graves Editorial Service, and Karen Hammon of Graphic Advantage, who have worked diligently to prepare these books for publication.

We would also like to deeply acknowledge the work of Marilyn Burns, Liping Ma, John Van De Walle, the National Council of Teachers of Mathematics, and the Trends In Math and Science Studies (TIMSS) researchers James Hiebert and Jim Stigler. Their individual and collective work have played a key role in developing the concepts and procedures upon which this framework is based.

Special thanks to all the leaders and educators across the United States who have attended the *Five Easy Steps to a Balanced Math Program* workshops and applied the steps in their own schools and districts. In particular, we want to recognize and thank five urban school districts that have made the *Five Easy Steps* framework their district-wide mathematics initiative of choice: Norfolk Public Schools in Norfolk, Virginia; the Metropolitan School District of Wayne Township in Indianapolis, Indiana; the Muscogee County School District of Columbus, Georgia; Villa Park District #45 in Villa Park, Illinois; and Dalton Public Schools in Dalton, Georgia.

Acknowledgments

Owing to the leadership and vision of Dr. Denise Walston, Norfolk Public Schools became the first major school district in the nation to adopt the Five Easy Steps model. Dr. Terry Thompson, Dr. Karen Gould, Michele Walker, and Dr. Lisa Lantrip of Wayne Township have continued to advocate and refine *Five Easy Steps* as their district math initiative for all elementary and junior high schools. Dr. Karen Greyor, Dr. Shelia Barefield, Dr. Maxine Lee, and Dr. Paula Shaw-Powell of Muscogee County Schools selected *Five Easy Steps* as the district's math framework for K–7 schools beginning with the 2005–06 school year. Dr. Susan Schwicardi of Villa Park District #45, near Chicago, first saw the potential for improving student achievement in math through the *Five Easy Steps* program several years ago and made it a district initiative at that time. Dr. Virginia Foley, Executive Director of Student Services in the school district of Dalton Public Schools, Dalton, Georgia, continues to advocate the implementation of the *Five Easy Steps* framework within her district's schools. We are sincerely grateful to these leaders and their educators for their diligence and commitment to this program that is improving student achievement in mathematics.

We also wish to thank and commend the Metropolitan School District of Lawrence Township in Indianapolis, Indiana. Under the leadership of Dr. Marcia Capuano, Dr. Jan Combs, and Dr. Walter Bourke, several of their elementary and all of their middle schools have implemented the *Five Easy Steps* model.

We would like to extend special thanks to the many math educators from across the country who gave us permission to publish their math performance assessment examples in Step 3.

About the Authors

Larry Ainsworth is the Executive Director of Professional Development at the Center for Performance Assessment in Englewood, Colorado. He travels widely throughout the United States to assist school systems in implementing best practices related to standards, assessment, and accountability across all grades and content areas. In addition to the three editions of *Five Easy Steps to a Balanced Math Program* (2006), Larry is the author or co-author of five other published books: *"Unwrapping" the Standards, Power Standards, Common Formative Assessments, Student-Generated Rubrics,* and *Five Easy Steps to a Balanced Math Program* (the last two co-authored with Jan Christinson). Larry's primary motivation is to assist educators and leaders in helping all students succeed by taking the mystery out of the instruction, learning, and assessment process.

Larry has delivered keynote addresses nationwide, most notably for the U.S. Department of Education, New York Department of Education, Ohio Department of Education, Michigan Department of Education, Connecticut Department of Education, Connecticut Technical High School System, Colorado Department of Education, Harvard University Graduate School of Education's Principals' Center, Indiana ASCD, Indiana Computer Educators' Conference, California ASCD, California Private Schools' Association, Ohio's Battelle for Kids Conference, University of Southern Maine, Virginia Title I and STARS conferences, and the Southern Regional Education Board. He has conducted breakout sessions at national and regional conferences throughout the country, most notably for the California Math Council, the California International Studies Project, the Alabama CLAS Summer Institute, the Delaware Professional Development Conference, the National Council of Teachers of Mathematics, the National Association for Supervision and Curriculum Development, and the National School Conference Institute.

With 24 years' experience as an upper elementary and middle school classroom teacher in demographically diverse schools, Larry brings a varied background and wide range of professional experiences to each of his presentations. He has held numerous leadership roles within school districts, including mentor teacher and K–12 math committee co-chair, and has served as a mathematics assessment consultant in several San Diego County school districts.

Larry holds a Master of Science degree in educational administration.

For questions or suggestions regarding the implementation of *Five Easy Steps to a Balanced Math Program,* please contact the author at:

Larry Ainsworth
Executive Director, Professional Development
Center for Performance Assessment
317 Inverness Way South, Suite 150
Englewood, CO 80112
800-844-6599 ext. 509
lainsworth@makingstandardswork.com

About the Authors

Jan Christinson is currently a Distinguished Teacher-in-Residence in the College of Education at California State University at San Marcos and a consultant for the Center for Performance Assessment located in Englewood, Colorado. He has 30 years of teaching experience at the elementary, middle school, and university levels, and has worked with school districts and teachers across the country to improve their classroom instruction in mathematics. In addition to the three editions of *Five Easy Steps to a Balanced Math Program* (2006), Jan has co-authored *Student-Generated Rubrics, Five Easy Steps to a Balanced Math Program* (with Larry Ainsworth), and *Writing Prompts for Middle School Mathematics*.

Throughout his teaching career, Jan has held various leadership positions, including mentor teacher, math department chair, K–12 math committee co-chair, and summer school principal. He presents assessment workshops for beginning teacher support groups in California and helps teacher candidates prepare for basic skills tests that are part of the teacher credentialing process. He has presented sessions at regional math conferences, and has participated in assessment projects for the San Diego County Office of Education.

Jan holds a masters degree in education.

For questions or suggestions regarding the implementation of *Five Easy Steps to a Balanced Math Program*, please contact the author at:

Jan Christinson
Professional Development Associate
Center for Performance Assessment
317 Inverness Way South, Suite 150
Englewood, CO 80112
800-844-6599 ext. 507
jchristinson@makingstandardswork.com

Introduction

The Need for a Balanced Math Program

How can teachers produce mathematically powerful students—
students who can solve problems and also communicate their
understanding to others? Our extensive experience as elementary
and middle school math teachers has proven that when students
are engaged in a "balance" of mathematics activities, they *can*
succeed where it counts: in applying their math skills and reasoning ability to solve real-life problems requiring mathematical
solutions. By *balance* we mean the deliberate design of instruction
and assessment that helps students:

Build computational skills

Develop mathematical reasoning and problem-solving abilities

Deepen conceptual understanding

Demonstrate understanding in a variety of assessment formats

Since the first edition of *Five Easy Steps to a Balanced Math Program:
A Practical Guide for K-8 Classroom Teachers* was published in 2000,
we have received an increasingly enthusiastic reception to this
framework in schools and districts we have worked with across the
nation. These five steps are practical, they make sense, and they
are easy to understand and implement. They are designed according
to recommendations for effective mathematics instruction and
assessment from some of the most highly regarded authorities
working in mathematics education today.

Busy teachers typically begin implementing these steps in the
order in which they are presented in the book. Once the teachers
have their Math Review and Mental Math practices (step 1) in place,

they introduce the problem-solving process (step 2), followed by the design of a conceptual unit focused on a particular math topic essential for student understanding (step 3). Because student mastery of math facts (step 4) is as important to success in mathematical procedures and reasoning as learning the alphabet is to reading and writing, elementary school faculties distribute or "map" the teaching of these facts across the grades, consciously planning so that students can master the facts *before* they enter middle school.

Periodically, grade-level teachers at the elementary level and course-specific teachers at the secondary level want to know how students are doing relative to a particular set of math standards that they are all teaching to their students. Hence, they design, administer, score, and analyze a common formative math assessment (step 5) at various intervals throughout the year to assess for learning, so that they can adjust and differentiate instruction to meet the diverse learning needs of their students. With the *Five Easy Steps* framework in mind, teachers implement, one by one, each of these five interconnected steps to produce mathematically powerful students!

We believe teachers are feeling the frustration of the times, wanting to provide their students with a strong math program but not really feeling confident in their ability to do so. Three challenges must be addressed:

1. *Many teachers have not received sufficient professional development in mathematics.*

   The result can be resistance to math programs that emphasize conceptual understanding over computational mastery. Without ongoing professional development in current methodology,

Introduction

educators often resort to teaching math by the familiar, procedure-driven way they learned when they themselves were students.

Achieving different results requires a different approach. Teachers need a new way to organize their math programs—a simple framework for teaching all the essential mathematical components—and the continuing support to confidently implement that framework.

2. *Many teachers feel that their district math programs are confusing, have too many components to include in a math lesson, and address too many standards to cover in the course of one school year.*

The result for these teachers can be the uncomfortable feeling that they are not doing enough, that there are too many learning objectives to work into each day's lesson, and that there is not enough time to do it all. The problem is compounded if these teachers have not received sufficient professional development to experience a paradigm shift in the way they view mathematics education, a shift that helps them:

- Encourage students to look for multiple ways to tackle a new problem
- Value students' understanding and the ability to communicate that understanding verbally and in writing
- Promote problem-solving skills and conceptual understanding over memorization of computational procedures and formulas.

In addition, many teachers perceive gaps or holes in their district-adopted math programs, and recognize the need to

Teachers need a new way to organize their math programs—a simple framework for teaching all the essential mathematical components—and the support to confidently implement that framework.

supplement the district programs with lessons and math activities from other sources. This further increases their anxiety over being able to accomplish everything students need for mathematical success.

To address this challenge, we suggest:

- An organizational structure for providing students with the necessary components of a balanced math program, regardless of the math series in use
- A framework for planning instruction that aligns instruction, learning activities, and assessments around a particular math focus

Working from a viewpoint based on balance, teachers can more effectively pace their instructional activities throughout the school year. They can confidently make their own instructional decisions rather than letting the teacher's edition of the textbook drive instruction. They can more effectively utilize the math textbook and select supplementary materials for specific instructional purposes when appropriate. In short, they can better meet the learning needs of *all* their students.

3. *Many teachers feel pressured to make sure that their students achieve satisfactory scores on high-stakes achievement tests, often at the expense of teaching math in ways they know will develop their students' conceptual understanding and problem-solving abilities.*

Too often, what results is a binary choice: *either* emphasize computational skills and memorization of formulas all year long, to prepare students to do well on the state tests; *or* deemphasize those tested skills so as to teach in-depth lessons designed to promote conceptual understanding. Teachers who choose the latter approach often resolve their accountability anxiety by reluctantly putting aside their conceptual math lessons for the month prior to the test, and substituting drill-and-kill instruction on what students are likely to be tested on.

We think the solution lies not in a binary choice of computation *or* conceptual understanding, but rather a blend of computation *and* conceptual understanding. Such a solution may seem intellectually obvious, yet for many teachers the question remains, *"How* do I effectively combine both?" Here is how we answered that question for ourselves.

We focus on math computation practice during the first part of *every* math lesson, to help students sharpen and maintain their math skills *over time.* This consistent, daily practice results in students retaining those skills, as opposed to the short-term (and short-lived) recall that comes from cramming for a test.

We then devote the remainder of the math lesson to conceptual understanding and problem solving. In this way, we prepare our students for the full range of multiple assessment measures they will eventually encounter, from the all-important state assessment to district and classroom assessments, while simultaneously providing them with the skills and understanding needed to successfully solve math-related problems throughout their lives.

Developing a balanced math program is the answer for teachers who want to ensure that their students are receiving the full range of mathematical understanding and skills. The purpose of this book is to share with other teachers the methods we have successfully developed for doing just this. We take readers step-by-step through each of the five steps in our balanced math

Developing a balanced math program is the answer for teachers who want to ensure that their students are receiving the full range of mathematical understanding and skills.

program model, describing in an easy-to-follow sequence how to implement the program successfully in secondary-grade classrooms.

Designing the Balanced Math Program

Five Easy Steps to a Balanced Math Program: A Practical Guide for K-8 Classroom Teachers (2000) introduced five essential components for developing an effective mathematics program. Based on the National Council of Teachers of Mathematics (NCTM) recommendations, the book provided math educators in elementary and middle schools with a practical framework for implementing each of these components.

As a result of presenting the *Five Easy Steps* seminar and assisting teachers in the implementation of these ideas over the past six years, we realized the need to update this information. We wanted to make it more specific to particular grade spans (K–2, 3–5, and 6–8) and to the individual grades within each of those grade spans. In addition, the framework proved equally relevant and useful for high school, particularly the first two years. For these reasons, we decided to publish three books—one each for the primary, upper elementary, and secondary grades—rather than one K–12 book as an expanded second edition. These three books are titled: *Five Easy Steps to a Balanced Math Program for **Primary** Grades; Five Easy Steps to a Balanced Math Program for **Upper Elementary** Grades;* and *Five Easy Steps to a Balanced Math Program for **Secondary** Grades.* Readers familiar with the original book will find that these new publications enhance their understanding of the five steps and show how to implement the steps more effectively within their classrooms and schools.

Introduction

The five main components of the *Five Easy Steps to a Balanced Math Program* are summarized here.

Step 1: Computational Skills (Math Review and Mental Math). **Math Review** emphasizes the development of number sense as students practice procedural mathematics and computational skills every day. It also prepares students for success on the annual state mathematics assessment. **Mental Math** helps students become skillful in computing math problems mentally.

Step 2: Problem Solving. This step provides both a structure for problem-solving activities related to the current conceptual unit focus and a general problem-solving rubric or scoring guide that is used throughout the year to assess student work.

Step 3: Conceptual Understanding. Step 3 begins by identifying, in district and state math standards, a particular grade-level or course topic that is essential for student understanding. That topic becomes the focus of a conceptual math unit that is deliberately designed to align instruction with an end-of-unit assessment.

Step 4: Mastery of Math Facts. The emphasis in step 4 is on fact recall through student understanding of patterns. A program of accountability enables students to learn all their basic math facts by the end of elementary school. The process begins with the faculty mapping all of the addition, subtraction, multiplication, and division facts across grades K–5 so that students enter middle school already knowing their math facts.

Step 5: Common Formative Assessment. The final step aligns school-based assessments *for* learning to math Power Standards. These formative assessments are collaboratively designed, administered, scored, and analyzed within each grade level several times throughout the school year. Common formative assessments provide teachers with valid feedback as to students' current understanding of the Power Standards in focus. Such data provide predictive value regarding how students are likely to perform on subsequent district and state assessments—in time for teachers to modify and adjust instruction to meet specific learning needs.

Organization of This Book

The book has been organized into three major parts. **Part One** describes each of the five steps and the application of each step to the secondary grade spans (6–8 and 9–12). Each of its five chapters includes:

Essential Questions with opportunity for reader reflection

Rationale from acknowledged mathematics authorities

Description of the particular step

Examples of the particular step and how to implement it

Development of the step through each of the secondary grades

Differentiation strategies

Reader's assignment

Part Two presents guidelines for implementing the balanced math program in grades 6, 7, and 8, and high school. Included in each of these three chapters are examples specific to that grade, along with practical suggestions for successful implementation.

Part Three offers time management suggestions and responses to frequently asked questions. In addition, we have included, in Chapter 10, recommended guidelines for school leaders to assist them in effectively implementing the five steps within their buildings.

The "Reproducibles" section contains reproducible versions of the templates presented throughout the chapters. These forms can be duplicated for school and classroom use.

As We Begin

We designed *Five Easy Steps to a Balanced Math Program for Secondary Grades* to serve as a road map for middle school and high school math teachers. We encourage you to make this information your own, either by following it to the letter or by adapting it in whatever ways best meet your own individual needs. Our sincere hope is that our model will make you eager to create a balanced math program in your own classroom! If you have any questions along the way, please do not hesitate to contact either of us at the addresses provided in the "About the Authors" section. Ready? Let's get started!

PART ONE

The Five Easy Steps

Step 1: Computational Skills
(Math Review and Mental Math)

CHAPTER **1**

Essential Questions

In what ways are you helping students retain math concepts and skills they have already been taught?

How are you helping students develop and refine their number sense?

We suggest taking a few minutes of personal reflection time to respond to these questions.

Rationale

Number sense is essential to student success with computational skills. The key to effective practice when learning any new concept or skill is timely and specific feedback. Providing students with a daily opportunity to reflect on their progress increases their responsibility for learning. Helping students become aware of their individual mistakes or misunderstandings increases their chance for math success.

Teachers also benefit from the practice of regularly reviewing and assessing students' computational skills. They become aware of students' common mistakes and misunderstandings so that they can appropriately modify and adjust instruction. They learn to emphasize computational skills that are meaning-based (making sense) rather than procedure-based (following formulas with little or no understanding).

Description of Step 1: Math Review Component

The first key component of a balanced math program is a simple system for reviewing basic computational skills on a daily basis; we call it "Math Review." During the first 15 minutes of every math class, students solve and process a set of five problems. These problems should:

Represent the specific standards for that grade level or course

Provide practice in several math standards or strands

Match the conceptual focus of the current instructional unit or set of lessons

Reinforce prior learning and retention of previously taught concepts and skills

Provide daily practice for the computation sections on district and state assessments

The purpose of Math Review is simply that: *review.* It is not to instruct students on *new* concepts and skills. However, regular review of and practice with basic concepts and skills, prior to formal instruction on those concepts and skills (described in Step 3: Conceptual Understanding), greatly enhance student understanding when these *are* taught during a focused set of lessons or unit of study later in the school year.

Math Review is the place in the math period to discuss with students reasonableness of answer and estimation. It is also the perfect opportunity to help students develop computational strategies and skills. Instead of teaching students a procedure that implies there is only one way to solve a problem, emphasize and model *multiple* approaches to solving problems. This fosters students' mathematical reasoning and develops their number sense. According to Marilyn Burns, nationally recognized mathematics authority, "Number sense encompasses a wide range of abilities, including being able to make reasonable estimates, think and reason flexibly, make sound numerical judgments, and see numbers as useful. Students with number sense have good numerical intuition" (1999, p. 408).

A Deliberate Selection of Problems

An effective Math Review session involves more than simply writing a different set of random math problems on the board each day. Instead, the teacher deliberately selects specific problems representing different math standards and then focuses student review and practice on variations of those same problems through-out the week. While students practice solving those problems each day, they receive additional guidance and instruction as needed from both the teacher and their peers.

If we want students to maximize their learning of particular math computational skills, we must avoid introducing them to new kinds of problems within the same week. It is far more effective to keep students focused on a few *types* of problems and then have students consistently practice those same types of problems until they learn how to do them.

Math Review establishes a deliberate progression of mathematical concepts and computational skills that increase in difficulty throughout the school year. Problems of the same type recur week after week until the majority of the class learns them. Only then does the teacher introduce a new type of problem to replace the

> *Math Review establishes a deliberate progression of mathematical concepts and computational skills that increase in difficulty throughout the school year.*

Step 1: Computational Skills
(Math Review and Mental Math)

*Math Review problems
for middle school students
should reflect state
standards, standardized
test items, and the
current unit of study.*

one that students have sufficiently learned. In this way, new types of problems are cycled through Math Review as the year proceeds.

If students need to revisit any concepts or skills at some point later in the year, those types of problems can again be included in Math Review. However, if students practice a particular computational concept or skill until they thoroughly understand it, teachers will find that they seldom need to completely re-teach that concept or skill in the future. They can better build on students' prior understanding when those concepts and skills appear again in more challenging problems or applications.

The Middle School Challenge

The challenge of middle school mathematics is to move students toward more complex mathematics while at the same time maintaining their basic math skills and their ability to determine a reasonable answer. Math Review problems for middle school students should reflect state standards, standardized test items, and the current unit of study. To successfully prepare students to understand algebra, Math Review problems must continually reinforce skills related to fractions, decimals, and percents. You will not succeed if you merely present isolated computational problems at the middle school level; the Math Review problems have to flow from and directly relate to the current conceptual unit and to the kinds of problems students will encounter on the state test.

Following are some ideas to consider when utilizing Math Review in the middle school classroom:

Emphasize fractions, decimals, and percents (again, very important to success in algebra).

Description of Step 1: Math Review Component

Be persistent and maintain the process *enthusiastically* (it pays off with this age group).

Watch the time and try to keep Math Review to about 15 minutes (it can easily take over your entire period if you are not careful).

Assess every *two* weeks (very important for this age group; a lot is happening in their lives, so they regularly need to know how they are doing).

Make sure numbers do not become cumbersome; keep computation reasonable to allow students to focus on the concept.

The Math Review Template

The Math Review Template shown in Figure 1.1 is an organizational structure we developed to implement this daily computational practice. It consists of five labeled boxes with a problem and accompanying work space in each. These problems target the current math concepts or skills the teacher wants students to focus on

Sample Secondary-Grades Math Review Template	Figure 1.1

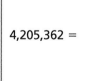

$$4,205,362 =$$

Place Value

$$\frac{1}{3} + \frac{1}{6} + \frac{1}{4} = \underline{\quad}$$

Fraction Operations

$$4.24 \times 3.4 = \underline{\quad}$$

Decimals

$$2^2 \times 2^3 = \underline{\quad}$$

Exponents

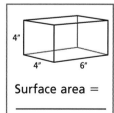

Surface area =

Geometry

during that two-week time frame. Often teachers include a bonus problem for early finishers, who often need an additional challenge. This bonus problem can be either a word problem that takes one or two steps to solve, or it can be a more difficult version of one of the regular Math Review problems.

For example, the sample secondary-grade template shown in Figure 1.1 targets five different math standards or focus topics. The sections that follow explain how we instruct students to solve these problems, as well as how we process the problems together after students have solved them. (*Note:* Specific examples of the Math Review template for grades 6, 7, and 8, and high school are provided in Part Two, "Inside the Secondary Classroom." Problems that are more appropriate for each individual grade level appear there.)

The Teacher's Role During Math Review

The teacher is critical to the success of Math Review. Students need to hear the teacher giving such encouragement as, "Math Review is a time for *practice*. We are all trying to get better at this, so let's help each other as much as possible."

While the students are working, the teacher circulates throughout the classroom and helps students individually, or invites those who are having difficulty with a particular problem to come forward to the board for individual or small-group assistance. Students can come and go after each problem, depending on their needs. These changing, informal groups, called *flex groups,* provide a safe place for students to seek the help they might otherwise not ask for. The teacher strives to create a collaborative atmosphere in which students are willing to risk and admit their need for help. The message is: "Learning is a process that begins with *not* knowing. As we practice and help each other, we come to understand."

Description of Step 1: Math Review Component

Processing Math Review

When the time for students to solve the Math Review problems (usually 10 minutes) has elapsed, the teacher and students correct the problems together. The processing of the Math Review problems should take approximately five minutes. The key to processing Math Review effectively is to emphasize number sense and reasonableness of answer and to do this *on a regular (daily) basis.* Processing Math Review helps students determine for themselves whether their own answers are reasonable and make sense, and if their answers demonstrate an understanding of our number system. Students in middle school and high school need to continue developing number-sense strategies, rather than merely learning procedural methods that emphasize rote memorization of formulas. The daily processing of the Math Review problems greatly assists them in doing so.

Teachers who strive to create a classroom climate in which mistakes are regarded as a normal part of the learning process make it much easier for students to want to improve. Students become more receptive to learning how to do an error analysis of their work when their Math Review answers are incorrect. This *error analysis* is a way to help students (1) identify the part of the problem done correctly and (2) pinpoint the part of the problem where they made an error. With this kind of daily practice in analyzing their math processes, students gain confidence in their mathematical ability and *do* improve.

When introducing a new concept or skill into the Math Review mix of problems, or when a majority of the class seems stuck on a particular problem, the teacher may lead the class through the step-by-step computational procedure, pointing out the critical elements and asking students for a reasonable answer. The teacher

> *The key to processing Math Review effectively is to emphasize number sense and reasonableness of answer and to do this on a regular (daily) basis.*

emphasizes the key points and encourages students to verbalize how they will use those key points to solve the problem from then on. Secondary-grade students are also encouraged to take notes on key points to help them remember how to solve such a problem on their own the next time they encounter a similar one.

Let's revisit the five sample problems illustrated in Figure 1.1 to describe how teachers can effectively process each one. Figure 1.2 shows an expansion of the Math Review problems with key processing points pertaining to each one.

Other Important Ways to Process Math Review

When introducing students to the processing of Math Review, we recommend that the teacher direct the process (as described earlier in this chapter) until students are familiar with the way it is done and can begin to use the process independently. However, there are several other ways to process Math Review and to conduct an error analysis; these are described in the following subsections. Note that these different ways are offered so that teachers can vary the way they process Math Review. Our intent is not to suggest that each teacher use each and every way presented every single day. Math Review should be fun, not overwhelming! These are merely different methods to effectively develop students' number sense. The teacher should select the methods that best meet the changing needs of the class. Be sure to emphasize with students (1) the most common mistake made on a particular type of problem; (2) reasonable answer; and (3) test-taking strategies. What is most important in the processing of Math Review is teaching students how to conduct their own error analysis. Teachers play a critical role in consistently modeling this process.

Description of Step 1: Math Review Component

$$4,205,362 =$$

Place Value

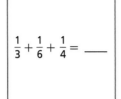

$$\frac{1}{3} + \frac{1}{6} + \frac{1}{4} = \underline{\quad}$$

Fraction Operations

$$4.24 \times 3.4 = \underline{\quad}$$

Decimals

$$2^2 \times 2^3 = \underline{\quad}$$

Exponents

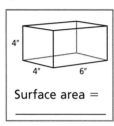

Surface area = _____

Geometry

Place Value

Key Points:

- Expanded notation (4,000,000 + 200,000 + 5,000 + 300 + 60 + 2)
- Saying number correctly
- *What number is 10 more; 100 more; 1,000 less; etc.?*
- *What do the commas tell you?*

Fraction Operations

Key Points:

- Emphasize *reasonable-answer* strategy using relative size of fraction (i.e., $\frac{1}{3} + \frac{1}{6} = \frac{1}{2}$, so $\frac{1}{2} + \frac{1}{4}$ is less than a whole)
- *Most common mistake* is that student adds numerators and denominators without use of common denominator
- More than/less than a whole (i.e., $\frac{1}{3} < 1$; $\frac{1}{4} < 1$; $\frac{1}{6} < 1$; how do you know?)
- Common denominator: *Why do we need a common denominator for the procedure?* (to be able to compare same-size pieces). Procedure works because of equivalent fractions

$$\frac{1}{3} + \frac{1}{6} + \frac{1}{4}$$
$$\frac{4}{12} + \frac{2}{12} + \frac{3}{12}$$

Decimals

Key Points:

- **Most common mistake** is that students don't know what to do with the decimal, so they bring it down to the answer or count over using their own invented or misunderstood strategy

- Emphasize *reasonable-answer* strategy using whole numbers: 4.24 (round to 4) multiplied by 3.4 (round to 3) $\approx$ 12
- Whole-number estimation to place decimal in answer: 4.24 (rounded to 4) multiplied by 3.4 (rounded to 3) $\approx$ 12 helps students place the decimal correctly (14.416)
- Saying numbers correctly ("four and twenty-four hundredths," not "four point two four")

Exponents

Key Points:

- Vocabulary (2^3; 2 is the base and 3 is the exponent)
- Expanded form ($2^2 = 2 \times 2$; $2^3 = 2 \times 2 \times 2$)
- Common base generalization (common base of 2; add the exponents 2 and 3 to get 5 (2^5))
- Expanded form proves generalization
- Reasonable answer/number sense ($2^2 = 4 \times 4 = 16 \times 2 = 32$)

Geometry

Key Points:

- Surface area is the measure of the outside faces of a shape expressed in square units
- Square units: *What is a square inch?*
- Faces: rectangular solids are made up of six faces in matching sets of two
- Generalization and pattern: If you find the top, you also know the bottom; if you find the front, you also know the back; if you find one end, you also know the other end
- Reasonable answer: Help students use their knowledge of the patterns within a rectangular solid to make a reasonable estimate of surface area

STUDENT-DIRECTED.   In this method, student volunteers explain to the class the procedure they followed to arrive at a solution to each of the Math Review problems. If other students used different approaches to reach the same solution, and the teacher decides it would benefit the rest of the class to see and/or hear them, the teacher may invite those students to share their approaches as well.

"PASS THE PEN."   This is a diagnostic tool we use when most of the students know how to do a particular kind of problem. It is an effective method to assist the teacher in seeing where students might have trouble with a particular part of a problem and to provide needed instruction. As one student demonstrates one step of the solution on the board or overhead projector, others watch to see if they agree or disagree. The student at the board then "passes the pen" (or marker, or chalk) to another student who must demonstrate the next step. This continues until the problem is solved and all agree that the answer is correct.

SPEEDY SYSTEM.   When students have become successful with the Math Review problems, volunteers go to the board and just write the answer to the problem. They then ask the class, "How many agree? How many disagree?" This enables the class to determine quickly whether or not their answers are correct.

ROW OR GROUP EXPERT.   The first student to finish in a student row or cooperative group begins to assist other students in that row or cooperative group with the day's assigned problems. During this time, the "expert" discusses solutions with other students in that row or group who have also completed the problems. Such conversations prove very helpful for students who have not yet mastered the concepts being presented.

Description of Step 1: Math Review Component

ROW OR GROUP REPRESENTATIVE. Assign each row or cooperative group of students a certain problem that they must solve and reach consensus on. After all students have completed the day's problems, the row or cooperative group representative shares with the class the group's answer to the assigned problem and describes how his or her group determined its answer.

MATH VOCABULARY. Encourage students to use related math vocabulary and write related number sentences next to the problems as they are solved and later shared with the whole class. Teachers often create a Math Word Wall of frequently used math vocabulary to assist students in incorporating correct mathematical terms into their oral and written work.

IDENTIFY MATH CONCEPTS. Ask students to identify key math concepts they are practicing in given problems. For example, to add unlike denominators in a fraction problem, students must understand the math concept of finding a common denominator to get similar-size pieces.

COMMON MISTAKE. Alert students to the most common mistake made on a particular problem, to help them avoid that mistake from then on. In another fraction example, a common mistake students make when adding unlike fractions is to just add the numerators together and the denominators together without first finding a common denominator. This typical mistake is often due to student misunderstanding of a procedure taught to them in prior years.

One cautionary note: Math Review provides such stimulating opportunities for teacher instruction and student learning that it can easily expand to encompass the entire time allocated for math!

A way to prevent this is to focus the Math Review processing on only two or three problems at first, and vary that focus each day. In this way, students will develop their number sense and conceptual understanding underlying the procedures, as well as reflect on their own learning; at the same time, the teacher will be able to stay within the recommended 20 minutes allotted to Math Review *and* Mental Math (described later in this chapter).

In the beginning of the year, or whenever teachers introduce any new process to students, the time required is naturally longer. However, strive to limit step 1 to about one-third of the total math session. Otherwise, the first step in your balanced math program will unbalance the other four!

Assessment: The Math Review Quiz

Essential Questions

How will you know if Math Review is effective?

How will you assess for *learning (gather information about student mistakes and misconceptions in order to differentiate instruction)?*

Rationale

Regular assessment of student progress is necessary to make Math Review effective. If students are to improve, teachers need insights regarding student misconceptions. Formative assessment results provide teachers with diagnostic information on a regular basis. Teachers use these results to differentiate instruction that should include intervention for struggling learners and enrichment or acceleration for more able learners. To know what instructional changes they need to make to meet the learning needs of all students, secondary-grade teachers administer a Math Review Quiz every other week.

In middle school and high school, this twice-monthly assessment provides teachers with the means to determine which students do and do not understand the computational problems they have been practicing throughout the prior two weeks. It provides both teachers *and* students with timely feedback and allows students the opportunity to reflect on their current performance, so as to plan for personal improvement. Again, the value of this biweekly assessment is that it is *formative*. If students do not demonstrate proficiency on certain items, teachers need to decide what they must do to assist students to solve them correctly.

This analysis of student results may also reveal the need for the teacher to remove particular types of problems from the daily Math Review and place them in the instructional component of a current or future math lesson. Remember, the purpose of Math Review is *review*—it is not intended for direct instruction. Alternatively, analyzing the results of the Math Review Quiz may reveal that the *types* of problems are appropriate, but the particular problems are too difficult for the majority of the students to solve independently. This adjustment can be made immediately to make the problems more accessible to students. In both cases, such formative assessment is used to *inform* instruction.

The Math Review Quiz

Once every other week (elementary grades administer this assessment weekly), teachers give students a 10-problem assessment called the Math Review Quiz. It consists of two problems for each of the five kinds of problems practiced during the preceding nine days. The reason for using two problems per concept or skill is diagnostic: If a student incorrectly solves one problem but gets the other one right, the teacher may determine that the student simply made a calculation error. If the student misses both problems, the teacher correctly interprets this as indicating a need for further instruction on that particular concept or skill. This biweekly assessment enables the teacher to differentiate daily instruction for students according to individual and collective student need.

To be considered proficient, students need to correctly solve at least eight out of the ten problems on the Math Review Quiz. Students who can demonstrate this level of proficiency on the quiz may, during the following two weeks, choose to do only the bonus problem provided daily, or to assist other students by acting as tutors or helpers. However, these students must take the next Math Review Quiz to show that they can still correctly solve these same kinds of problems. Once new types of problems are cycled in, all students should complete the daily Math Review practice problems.

A Sample Math Review Quiz

Figure 1.3 is an example of a Math Review Quiz that matches the five-problem Math Review sample given in Figure 1.1. There are two problems for each type of problem the students practiced during the daily Math Review.

Scoring the Math Review Quiz

It is important that students receive immediate and specific feedback regarding their performance on the Math Review Quiz. Because of the large number of students they teach each day,

Sample Math Review Quiz	Figure 1.3

1. $5,206,354 =$ _____   **7.** $3^2 \times 3^3 =$ _____

2. $6,470,263 =$ _____   **8.** $4^3 \times 3^4 =$ _____

3. $\frac{1}{2} + \frac{1}{4} + \frac{1}{8} =$ _____

4. $\frac{2}{3} + \frac{1}{6} + \frac{1}{4} =$ _____

4″   2″   6″

5. $4.76 \times 2.3 =$ _____   **9.** Find the surface area.

6. $5.5 \times 4.5 =$ _____   **10.** Find the volume.

secondary-grade teachers typically have students exchange papers and correct the quizzes in class. Using a red marking pen, students star an answer if correct and check it if incorrect. When the papers are returned to their owners, students can see firsthand where they are doing well and where they need to improve.

Math Review Quiz Self-Reflection

After receiving their scored papers, students now reflect on their performance. Next to any incorrect answers, they write a phrase about why they missed that particular problem. They then turn over their papers to write a brief self-reflection that addresses their current Math Review Quiz performance, along with a simple plan for improvement during the next two weeks. *Note:* Teachers of special education students with writing challenges and English-language learners can follow these guidelines by asking students to reflect orally on their performance. As soon as students are able to write independently, however, we do ask them to complete their self-reflection as described here.

The effectiveness of this self-reflection process depends on the classroom teacher emphasizing the appropriate use of student errors and misunderstandings during the Math Review processing each day. As teachers help students begin to see errors as providing important information to know about their learning process—an assessment *for* learning—instead of being a negative reflection of their mathematical ability, students improve their performance. This active self-reflection helps learners focus on personal goals for improvement just before they begin a new week of Math Review.

Tutors and Tutees

Another successful method we use to build a supportive classroom atmosphere and meet the varying needs of all students is "Tutors and Tutees," a student–student partnership so named by Scott Koopsen, a teacher from Carlsbad, California. The *tutors* are peer helpers who volunteer to provide assistance to other students during Math Review. The *tutees* are students who are struggling with one or more computational skills as indicated either by their daily Math Review practice sessions and/or their performance on the biweekly Math Review Quiz. To become eligible to be a tutor, a student must correctly solve eight out of ten problems on the quiz. During the following two weeks, these students may then assist other students (the tutees) who scored lower than eight during the Math Review daily practice. However, *all* students must take the next Math Review Quiz.

Very often students can learn computational strategies more effectively from their peers than from their teachers. Having tutors work with tutees also provides teachers with needed assistance when many students ask for help at the same time. Because the teacher has organized Math Review to take advantage of students' ability to assist one another, students who need help get it when they need it, and thus are less likely to continue struggling unaided as the year progresses.

A word of caution is needed here, however. It is important to challenge tutors who can successfully solve the Math Review problems to do *more advanced* work, rather than just assist other students week after week. Even though they certainly gain great benefits by coaching or teaching other students, students who are proficient at Math Review must also be encouraged to tackle problems that challenge them mathematically. The daily bonus problem that accompanies the regular Math Review problems closely relates to the computational focus of the five problems the class is practicing during any given two weeks, but it should be more rigorous and extend student understanding of one or more of those kinds of problems.

The Home Connection and Extra Practice

Students take home their evaluated quizzes for parents to review and sign. This biweekly accountability informs parents of the actual progress their child is making in math computation. If students score less than 80%, parents may try to help them practice problems like those missed on the quiz.

To assist the parents in doing this, teachers typically send home practice problems to be completed for homework. The next morning, the teacher quickly checks to see if students have completed and returned the practice problems. By consistently monitoring the completion of this extra practice, the teacher communicates high

Students take home their evaluated quizzes for parents to review and sign. This biweekly accountability informs parents of the actual progress their child is making in math computation.

If a majority of the class falls below the 80% score, the teacher needs to reevaluate student understanding during Math Review and to make instructional adjustments accordingly.

expectations to both students and parents and establishes a standard of accountability.

During Math Review, the teacher works with these same students one-on-one or in a small flex group to make sure they receive additional instruction and assistance. This combined effort—the teacher's extra help during Math Review and students' practice at home—has proven quite successful for students who struggle with computation.

For certain students, help at home is not possible or not available. To respond to this reality, we pair these students with peers or teacher aides who help them practice at school. Depending on the unique circumstances at each school, the teachers and administrators must establish their own internal support system for helping these students before, during, and/or after the regular school day.

Benefits of the Math Review Quiz

The Math Review Quiz provides the teacher with a biweekly formative assessment that:

Identifies students who need remediation or intervention

Identifies students who need enrichment or acceleration

Gauges the effectiveness of computational instruction

If only a few students score below 80% on the biweekly quiz, those students can be taught individually or in small groups until they improve. If a majority of a class falls below the 80% score, the teacher needs to reevaluate student understanding during Math Review and to make instructional adjustments accordingly. In this way, assessment serves its most important function, that of informing instruction.

Examples of biweekly Math Review Quizzes aligned to daily Math Review problems are included in the specific grade-level implementation chapters of Part Two.

Differentiation

The following are general guidelines and suggestions for meeting the diverse learning needs of students at various ability levels within the classroom. Certain of these suggestions have been described throughout this chapter. However, we have included them again here along with additional strategies.

FLEXIBLE GROUPING. Using the data from the biweekly Math Review Quiz, along with informal observation and assessment, teachers create small student "flex groups." Place those students who continually have difficulty during Math Review into a group that will receive daily help from the teacher. As individual students start experiencing success in Math Review or begin to demonstrate their improved understanding on the Math Review Quiz, have them rejoin the class as a whole to work independently. Other students in need of direct assistance from the teacher can join the group until such time as they too are able to work successfully on their own.

PEER ASSISTANCE. Match students who show success on Math Review (tutors or helpers) with students who are struggling. During daily Math Review, these student pairs work together to complete the problems. Encourage the use of appropriate manipulatives to assist struggling students to understand the particular concepts and skills that are causing difficulty.

BONUS PROBLEM. Each day, provide students who are already proficient at the concepts and skills being presented with a bonus problem that involves more difficult mathematics. Teachers often include a sixth box on the Math Review template for a daily bonus problem. This bonus problem can be either a word problem or a more challenging version of any one of the five regular problems. The bonus problem engages students who finish the regular problems before others. It is also an excellent way to differentiate instruction for students who are ready for more advanced concepts or skills.

ENGLISH-LANGUAGE LEARNERS. Provide students who are learning English with peer assistance, and emphasize vocabulary development during the processing of the Math Review problems. Post key mathematical vocabulary in the classroom on a Math Word Wall. Emphasize vocabulary during the daily practice of Mental Math (as described in the next section), and include writing during Math Review on a daily basis.

ERROR ANALYSIS (TEACHER). Keep track of the concepts that are most problematic for students. Emphasize those concepts repeatedly during Math Review processing activities, as well as during Mental Math.

INDIVIDUAL ASSISTANCE. Find times during the day to offer struggling students one-on-one assistance. This may include meeting with these students before or after school, during lunch, or during breaks. Even a few minutes of individual work with a student can make a huge difference in that student's mathematical understanding.

Description of Step 1: Mental Math Component

Essential Questions

How are you providing students daily mental practice with number sense?

How are you providing opportunities for students to develop their own strategies for doing math problems in their heads?

Rationale

Students need regular opportunities to develop effective computational strategies that are based on number sense. Helping students use number strategies that they find comfortable and accurate is an effective way to develop number sense. Students need daily mental practice to develop and retain strong number sense and effective computational skills.

Cathy L. Seeley, president of the National Council of Teachers of Mathematics (NCTM), in her December 2005 "President's Message" to members, emphasizes the importance of learning to compute mentally:

> *In my observation, mental math does not receive the attention it deserves. Perhaps this is because the development of mental techniques is not always explicitly stated as an objective or state-level standard. Whatever the reason, the time has come to invest in helping students build the mental math skills in their tool kits as part of their comprehensive mathematical understanding. The payoff for this investment can be tremendous both in improving students' mathematical abilities and in giving a visible sign that we are committed to preparing students with the kind of mathematical proficiency that the public can readily appreciate.*

The purpose of Mental Math is to provide students with mental practice in computing basic number facts and combining mathematical operations.

How to Implement Mental Math

The second part of step 1 is Mental Math, a three-problem, computational workout for the brain that students love doing. Mental Math takes about five minutes of class time and immediately follows the processing of the Math Review problems. However, teachers report that they have found other times during the math period or math block in which to allow students to practice Mental Math.

The purpose of Mental Math is to provide students with *mental* practice in computing basic number facts and combining mathematical operations. The teacher selects a particular math theme or combination of themes and then dictates a string of numbers and operations that students compute mentally to determine the final answer.

Typical themes for Mental Math in the secondary grades include:

Number operations

Number properties

Fractional operations and concepts

Course-specific concepts, skills, and definitions

Math vocabulary

Concepts and skills specific to high-school exit exams

Reasonable answer

Exponents

Square roots

Description of Step 1: Mental Math Component

Percent-decimal-fraction equivalency

Measurement (metric and customary)

Statistical concepts (mean, median, mode, and so on)

After selecting one or more themes for Mental Math, the teacher then prepares a corresponding number string to dictate orally to the class. For example, to help students practice understanding the themes of exponents and square roots, the teacher could prepare and dictate the following number string:

Start with square root of 144 (12); add square root of 81 (21); divide by 7 (3); cube the result (27); add 3 (30); multiply by 4; equals . . . .

Pause briefly after each operational step. At each pause, students have a chance to calculate mentally before the teacher moves on to the next step, but they do not write anything down until the final answer. In the example, students calculate the answer in their heads and write "120" (we hope!) in their math journals right beneath the Math Review problems of the day.

The answer is not given yet, however. The teacher repeats the same problem to allow students who might need a second chance to succeed. Those students who think they know the correct answer are asked to calculate again "just to make sure." The teacher then asks the students to say the answer aloud together. The answer is verified by computing the problem aloud in increments to help those remaining students who still were unable to do it. In this way, everyone stays involved. By keeping everyone engaged in this way, the teacher helps students see how the answer was determined, and encourages those who are struggling to try the next problem.

Classes can usually accomplish three Mental Math problems in five minutes once students are familiar with the procedure. Choose the number of problems that is appropriate for your class and available time. Use problems that are fairly easy when first introducing this activity to students. You can make the problems more challenging as the year progresses and your students' confidence and ability improve.

Students often want to create their own Mental Math problems to dictate to the rest of the class. We always encourage this kind of involvement. However, before allowing these volunteers to say their problems aloud, students must write out the number string and have the teacher check it for appropriateness of difficulty (often student-created strings are too long and convoluted). We have also found it a good practice to write down the problem before saying it aloud. More than once, we've been unable to repeat the number string exactly, causing a minor uproar in the classroom!

A teacher in Louisiana came up with a wonderful way to engage students in learning math vocabulary terms while practicing Mental Math problems. She writes a new math term, with its definition, on a sentence strip and places that sentence strip somewhere on the wall in her classroom. For example, to reinforce the term *quadrilateral,* she writes on the strip, "A quadrilateral = 4-sided geometric shape." During Mental Math that day, she incorporates that term in her number string like this: "Start with the number of sides on a quadrilateral; square that number; add the number of centimeters in a meter; . . ." and so on. Each day or two she introduces a new math vocabulary term in the same way. During the *Five Easy Steps* workshop, she reported that her students began coming into class each day looking for the new math term, knowing that she would use it during Mental Math. In this ingenious way, the teacher motivated her students to learn new math vocabulary; for them, it became a fun kind of game.

Mental Math Benefits

Practice doesn't always make perfect, but doing Mental Math daily throughout the school year helps all students achieve dramatic improvement. It provides students with regular opportunities to apply properties and patterns of our number system.

Many excellent commercial sources for Mental Math are available, but we find that teachers and students alike enjoy making them up themselves once they become familiar with the process. Sample Mental Math problems are included in each of the grade 6, grades 7 and 8, and high school implementation chapters to provide readers with a model for doing so.

Practice doesn't always make perfect, but doing Mental Math daily throughout the school year helps all students achieve dramatic improvement.

Reader's Assignment

Rather than waiting until the end of this book to begin planning how to implement these suggestions for creating a balanced math program in your own classroom, you may wish to put this information to use immediately and plan as you go. We have therefore included a Reader's Assignment at the end of each of the five steps to guide you (and your grade-level or teaching colleagues) through the step-by-step process of planning your own balanced program.

Step 1: Computational Skills
(Math Review and Mental Math)

Plan your own grade-level Math Review template, sample Math Review problems, and sample Mental Math problems. Refer to your particular classroom chapter (grade 6, grades 7 and 8, or high school) in Part Two. Examples in these grade-specific chapters will assist you in planning your first daily Math Review problems, Mental Math problems, and Math Review Quiz. Refer also to Chapter 9 for answers to frequently asked questions about step 1, Computational Skills (Math Review and Mental Math).

Step 1 Products

Create a Math Review template for your grade level or course

Include sample Math Review problems

Prepare a sample Math Review Quiz

Create a few sample Mental Math problems appropriate for your grade level or course

Consider

What plans do you have for implementing Math Review and Mental Math?

Number of days per week?

Number of problems?

Template you will use?

Assessment or Math Review Quiz you will give?

Next steps you will take?

Step 2: Problem Solving

CHAPTER 2

Essential Questions

How are you providing opportunities for students to apply and explain their mathematical reasoning?

How are you including writing in your math program?

Rationale

The National Council of Teachers of Mathematics' *Principles and Standards for School Mathematics* (2000) states that students should be able to:

Organize and consolidate their mathematical thinking through communication

Communicate mathematical thinking coherently and clearly to others

Analyze and evaluate the mathematical thinking and strategies of others

Use the language of mathematics to express mathematical ideas precisely

Marilyn Burns emphasizes the chief benefits that both students and teachers realize when writing is incorporated into mathematics:

> *Writing in math class supports learning because it requires students to organize, clarify, and reflect on their ideas—all useful processes for making sense of mathematics. In addition,*

Step 2: Problem Solving

Our underlying purpose in asking students to communicate their thinking in both oral and written forms is to teach students how to explain their process to others.

when students write, their papers provide a window into their understandings, their misconceptions, and their feelings about the content they're learning (2004, p. 30).

In the same article, Burns shares key strategies teachers can use to incorporate writing (2004, p. 33):

1. Establish the purposes of writing in math class.

2. Establish yourself (the teacher) as the audience.

3. Ask students to include details and to explain their thinking as thoroughly as possible.

4. Post useful mathematics vocabulary.

5. Have students share their writing in pairs or small groups.

Problem solving gives students opportunities to *apply* their math skills and concepts. Student writing also provides diagnostic information for the teacher. As students develop experience with problem solving, they gain confidence and experience success.

The problem-solving step of a balanced math program provides students with a dual opportunity:

1. To apply the mathematics they are learning in the Conceptual Understanding Unit of instruction (described in step 3) to a problem-solving situation

2. To communicate their mathematical thinking to others

Mathematics and language processes are interrelated. Our underlying purpose in asking students to communicate their thinking in both oral and written forms is to teach students how to explain their *process* to others. In doing this, students develop the ability to think logically and follow the sequence of mental steps needed to solve math-related problems in real life.

Description of Step 2

We recognize that some students automatically compute mentally and are able to arrive at the answer quite quickly. Often, though, when teachers ask these students how they solved the problem, the reply is, "I just figured it out in my head" or "My brain told me." Other students are never quite sure how to approach a problem if it is not already in an arithmetic or algorithmic format. Because our goal is to produce mathematically powerful students who can reason, solve, and explain both procedural and application problems, we need to set up learning experiences through which students become able to articulate the mathematical process they followed—first for themselves, then for others.

Description of Step 2

Selecting the Problem-Solving Task

In the first stage of developing students' problem-solving skills, we introduce students to the *process* of mathematically showing how to solve a complex word problem requiring more than one step. The Problem-Solving Task gives students the opportunity to practice doing this. The task is a carefully selected problem matched to the current instructional unit or set of lessons that students discuss, solve, and write about during one or more class sessions.

When selecting a particular problem for students to solve, we look for one that will allow them to demonstrate their ability to apply the math they are learning to a real-world problem or situation. To assist us in doing this, we refer to the guiding questions listed on the next page.

Step 2: Problem Solving

Does this problem promote application of the mathematical ideas presented in the current instructional focus or unit of study?

Does this problem match students' current instructional level?

Is this problem accessible to all students?

Is the problem relevant and engaging to students?

Does this problem require students to "stretch" their mathematical reasoning abilities?

Does this problem involve more than one strand or standard of mathematics?

Is there more than one way to solve the problem?

Could the problem be extended or enriched?

Do *I* fully understand the mathematics in this problem, so that I can better facilitate student understanding?

With these guiding questions in mind, teachers can use the problem-solving resources provided in their math textbook series and supplemental math resource materials to select worthwhile mathematical tasks for students. Many excellent sources for problem-solving tasks are now available online (in particular, mathforum.org). Please refer to the math Webliography provided in the "References and Other Resources" section at the end of this book. In addition, we recommend *Nonfiction Writing Prompts for Math for Middle School* (Christinson, 2005), one of the books in the Write to Know series from Advanced Learning Press.

Teaching Students to Solve the Problem-Solving Task

Once we select the problem that will become the Problem-Solving Task, we follow a specific instructional sequence to teach students how to mathematically solve an application problem and communicate orally and in writing the process they used. Our ultimate goal for secondary-grade students is for them to be able to solve—independently—a multistep problem and to communicate verbally and in writing the process they used.

With that goal in mind, we first model the process for the whole class until students are familiar with the steps and can accomplish them independently. Next, we have students solve the selected problem in cooperative groups or teams. Once they are able to do this, we partner students to solve the given problem together. Lastly, we expect students to be able to complete the entire process independently. In the following subsections, we describe each of these stages in more detail.

WHOLE-CLASS INSTRUCTION. The teacher first introduces the Problem-Solving Task to the class and helps students understand its connection to the current instructional unit focus. He or she then guides students to solve the problem using calculation and/or graphic representation (words, pictures, and/or numbers). Here is a sequence of suggested steps for doing just that:

1. Teacher and students read the problem together. The teacher makes sure that students understand what the problem is asking.

2. Students take 5 to 10 minutes to attempt to solve the problem individually, using manipulatives if appropriate.

> *Our ultimate goal for secondary-grade students is for them to be able to solve—independently—a multistep problem and to communicate verbally and in writing the process they used.*

3. Students record their individual work on paper.

4. Students share possible strategies for solving the problem.

5. Teacher and students decide on a solution to the problem.

6. Teacher creates a class *Data Sheet*—a chart showing all the work done to solve the problem, usually represented with calculations and/or graphic representation.

7. Students copy the class Data Sheet.

8. Teachers and students compose a few sentences to describe how the problem was solved.

9. Teacher records the sentences on chart paper to be posted in the classroom.

10. Students copy the class-written explanation.

COOPERATIVE TEAMS.   Once students are familiar with the problem-solving process just described, the teacher arranges students into small, cooperative groups or teams. Guided by the teacher, students attempt to solve a new problem—without teacher assistance. Using computation and/or graphic representation the students complete a Data Sheet (again, our term for the work students do to solve the problem) and then copy their work onto easel-size chart paper. The members of the group then share the team's solutions with the rest of the class. The group members explain the process they followed and try to convince the class that their answer is correct and makes sense. Different teams will describe their processes differently and thus add to everyone's understanding of how to solve the problem. The class and teacher then discuss the different solutions presented and determine the actual answer.

Description of Step 2

This reporting activity enables the teacher to provide further instructions as to how the Data Sheet is to be done and to respond to student questions. This modeling is critical to ensuring students' long-term understanding and success on the second part of the process, the Problem-Solving Task Write-Up (described in the next section).

Once the presentations are finished, students display their chart-paper posters on the board or around the classroom as examples of their cooperative team problem solving. They will later refer to these models to assist them in completing subsequent Data Sheets for new problems. Teachers exchange existing posters for new ones each time the class completes a new Problem-Solving Task. This maintains student interest in problem solving all year long.

THE PROBLEM-SOLVING TASK WRITE-UP GUIDE. Because we want students to be able to communicate their mathematical process in writing, we now provide them with a format for doing so. The Problem-Solving Task Write-Up Guide establishes an organized structure through which students explain the mathematical work they have represented on their group Data Sheets. A sample write-up guide that includes the directions for both the Data Sheet and the written explanation is shown in Figure 2.1. When introducing this process to middle school or high school students, teachers can use this format (designed for upper elementary grades) or create their own, depending on the grade and ability levels of their students. Often middle school math teachers will use the more structured upper elementary guide until their students are ready to transition to the secondary Problem-Solving Task Write-Up Guide (Figure 2.2). Teachers who do decide to use the upper elementary template at first will

The Problem-Solving Task Write-Up Guide establishes an organized structure through which students explain the mathematical work they have represented on their group Data Sheets.

Figure 2.1	Problem-Solving Task Write-Up Guide (Secondary Grades)

PROBLEM-SOLVING TASK WRITE-UP GUIDE: MIDDLE SCHOOL AND HIGH SCHOOL

Data Sheet:

1. Head a piece of paper with your name, the date, the title of the problem (if given), and the words "Data Sheet."

2. Show *all* the work you did to solve the problem, using computation and/or graphic representation (words, pictures, and/or numbers).

3. Number each step as you work to solve the problem.

4. Write a number sentence that matches the problem.

5. Write a word sentence at the end of your Data Sheet that states the answer to the problem.

Write-Up:

Head a separate piece of paper:

1. Write your name, the date, and the title of the problem (if given), and the words "Write-Up" at the top of this paper.

2. Copy the title of each paragraph before you write your sentences for that paragraph.

3. Use the space below to complete your write-up. Everything you write must refer to the **math content, procedures you followed,** and **strategies you used** to solve the problem.

Paragraph One: Problem Statement

This problem is called _____ . It is about _____ .
I'm supposed to find _____ .

Paragraph Two: Work Write-Up

(It is understood that you have first read the problem and circled or underlined the key words. Do not include these steps in your write-up.) Explain **step by step,** in detail, everything you did **mathematically** to complete your Data Sheet and arrive at your answer. Refer back to your numbered steps on the Data Sheet to help you. Write this as if you were writing a recipe for someone to follow or giving a friend exact directions to your house. Use as many of these transition words as you need to describe each of your math steps: *first, next, then, after that, finally.*

Paragraph Three: Answer

My answer is _____ . I think my answer makes sense because _____ .
(Verify or prove your answer by referring to the *math* you did. It is not enough just to write that you checked it on the calculator, or that you checked it twice, or that a friend or parent or teacher told you so.)

Description of Step 2

PROBLEM-SOLVING TASK WRITE-UP GUIDE: MIDDLE SCHOOL AND HIGH SCHOOL

1. **Problem Statement:**
   Rewrite the problem in your own words so that someone reading your paper could understand exactly what you were asked to do. Be sure to include the question you want to answer.

2. **Plan:**
   Tell what you will do to solve the problem. Which strategy or strategies will you use? Before you begin work, develop a reasonable answer to the problem.

3. **Work:**
   Show *all* the work you did to solve the problem on your Data Sheet. Use a table, graph, picture, chart, and/or calculations. Explain in detail what you did so that the reader will understand your work and how you arrived at an answer.

4. **Answer:**
   Write your answer to the problem in a sentence. Verify your answer using mathematics. Could there be any other answers? Compare your answer to the reasonable estimate you made in step 2. Write what you learned from this problem that could help you to solve other problems.

Source: Adapted from Arlette Byrne, Valley Middle School, Carlsbad Unified School District, Carlsbad, CA.

certainly want to remove any references to "Upper Elementary" before giving it to their students, as we have done in Figure 2.1.

The middle school and high school Problem-Solving Guide in Figure 2.2 is less structured than the upper elementary template, but more rigorous in its demands. Its open-endedness is more compatible with the complex problem-solving tasks assigned to students at the secondary level, and allows more detailed written explanations.

Regardless of the write-up guide used, a very helpful strategy that enables students to transfer their recorded work from the Data

Step 2: Problem Solving

Regardless of when teachers begin this process with students, the benefits of teaching them how to solve word problems and communicate their processes are significant.

Sheet to the write-up guide is to number each of their steps as they complete their Data Sheets. In this way, they have only to look at the numbered Data Sheet and write a corresponding sentence or two that describes each numbered step. This simple strategy prevents students from writing: "First I read the problem. Then I thought about it. Next I worked it out. After that, I got my answer. Finally, I turned in my paper." Instead, their written work describes the actual *math steps* they followed to solve the problem. Note, too, that certain problems may not require five sentences to describe the actual math steps (one for each of the listed transition words), or they may require more than five. Instruct students to write as many sentences as they need *according to the numbered steps* on their Data Sheets, using transition words as needed.

INDEPENDENT STUDENT WORK. When the teacher decides that all students have had sufficient modeling, practice, and peer support in completing a Data Sheet and the corresponding write-up in cooperative groups and then with individual partners, he or she assigns a new Problem-Solving Task and asks students to try completing a Data Sheet and corresponding write-up independently. The teacher reviews the work students complete on their own to determine if further clarification and instruction are needed. Once students demonstrate that they understand and can follow the process independently, the teacher can confidently assign a Problem-Solving Task to be completed by students *on their own*.

This accomplishes the goal we set earlier in the year: to enable students to do this process independently. Regardless of when teachers begin this process with students, the benefits of teaching them how to solve word problems and communicate their processes are significant. Regular practice will enable students to analyze and solve a multiple-step problem—a critical skill for success in school, in everyday life, and on high-stakes assessments of their mathematical reasoning and problem-solving abilities.

Problem-Solving Strategies

The following is a list of strategies that students use to solve word problems:

Guess and check

Act it out

Work backward

Draw a graphic representation

Make a table, chart, or graph

Make a list

Write a number sentence, equation, or formula

Use logical reasoning

Find a pattern

To become successful problem solvers, students need practice with these strategies until the strategies become part of students' problem-solving toolkits. A note of caution is appropriate here, however. Most real-life problem-solving situations, and problems that appear on state assessments, do not neatly match one particular strategy from the preceding list. Students need to realize that knowing a *variety* of problem-solving strategies will better equip them to become confident problem solvers and use strategies appropriate to the given situation.

Problem-Solving Steps for Secondary Students

This section lists problem-solving steps to share with students. Teachers can make a chart of these to post in the classroom and then follow as a guide when modeling for students how to solve a word problem. This chart (which appears again in the "Reproducibles" section at the end of this book) can be duplicated for students to keep in their math folders or notebooks. Students who did not receive a strong problem-solving foundation during their elementary school years will benefit from learning a series of steps to use in analyzing and solving multiple-step problems.

GET READY TO SOLVE THE PROBLEM.

1. Read the problem first.

2. Underline or circle the important facts and key words.

3. What are you supposed to find out?

4. Are there any "tricky" parts to the problem?

5. What math vocabulary words are in the problem?

6. Which math strategies will you use?

7. What math tools might help you solve the problem?

SOLVE THE PROBLEM.

1. Solve the problem using calculation and/or graphic representation (words, pictures, and/or numbers).

2. Number each of your problem-solving steps (1, 2, 3, . . .) on your Data Sheet.

3. Write a number sentence, equation, and/or formula to match the problem.

4. Write an explanation to match each of your steps on the Data Sheet.

5. Prove or verify your answer.

WRITE HOW YOU SOLVED THE PROBLEM.

1. Find the first math step you did on your Data Sheet (the step labeled #1).

2. Write one or two sentences that explain what you did.

3. Find the second math step you did on your Data Sheet (the step labeled #2).

4. Write one or two sentences that explain what you did.

5. Continue this way until you have written one or more sentences for each of the other numbered math steps, using transition words (*next, then, after that, finally*) as needed.

6. Include math vocabulary appropriate to the problem or task.

7. Check each sentence to make sure it describes a *math step*.

8. Check to make sure each sentence makes sense.

WANT A BONUS CHALLENGE?

1. Can you add the word *because* after each math step you write and then explain why you did that step?

2. Can you include other math vocabulary words to help explain how you solved the problem?

3. Can you solve the problem in more than one way?

4. Can you find someone who solved it differently than you did?

5. Can you change the problem to make it more challenging?

6. Can you solve your own challenging problem?

7. Can you find someone else who will try to solve your problem?

Step 2: Problem Solving

The goal of step 2 in a balanced math program is to demonstrate for students how to communicate their mathematical understanding by following a specific format and using a specific procedure for doing so.

Figure 2.3 shows an example of a multistep Problem-Solving Task, with an accompanying Data Sheet and write-up, that is appropriate for the middle school grades. We chose this problem because it meets the criteria listed in the guiding questions for problem selection (listed earlier in this chapter). In addition, the student response can be regarded as an exemplar. Readers will find a Problem-Solving Task appropriate for grade 6, grades 7 and 8, and high school students in Chapters 6, 7, and 8, respectively. In addition, Chapter 9 sets out a weekly teaching schedule that includes a Problem-Solving Task and the other components of our balanced math program model.

An Investment of Time

It is important not to rush the process of teaching students to independently complete the Problem-Solving Task Data Sheet and write-up. A thorough job of initial instruction, combined with sufficient classroom practice, will prevent many future headaches for both teachers and students. While showing students how to correctly complete their first Data Sheets and write-ups, the teacher not only models the correct process for students to follow, but also emphasizes the correct use of mathematical vocabulary, clear mathematical reasoning, and verification of solution.

The goal of step 2 in a balanced math program is to demonstrate for students how to communicate their mathematical understanding by following a specific format and using a specific procedure for doing so. If teachers invest the time needed to teach their students to truly understand and apply this process, they will see wonderful results for their efforts: students who can apply mathematical concepts and procedures to real-world situations.

Secondary Problem-Solving Student Work Sample	Figure 2.3

AT THE ZOO

The keeper of the bird cages at the zoo discovered that two crested cockatoos would eat two pounds of bird seed every two weeks; that three Peruvian parrots would eat three pounds of bird seed every three weeks; and that four Mozambique macaws would eat four pounds of bird seed every four weeks. How many pounds of bird seed will 12 crested cockatoos, 12 Peruvian parrots, and 12 Mozambique macaws eat in 12 weeks?

Data Sheet
Jorge   Period 2

Crested Cockatoos

2 birds   2 birds x .5 = 1 bird

2 weeks   2 lbs x .5 = 1 lb.

2 lbs. food

       1 bird eats 1 lb. of food in two weeks, .5 lb. of food in 1 week

       .5 lb. x 12 weeks = 6 lbs. of food in 12 weeks

           x 12 birds
           ———————
           72 lbs. of food

Peruvian Parrots

3 birds   1 bird = 1 lb. = 3 weeks

3 lbs. food   x 4
              ———————
3 weeks   12 weeks

      12 ÷ 3 = 4

      1 bird = 4 lbs. food in 12 weeks

      12 birds x 4 lbs. = 48 lbs. of food in 12 weeks

(continues)

Figure 2.3 *(Continued)*	**Secondary Problem-Solving Student Work Sample**

Data Sheet (Continued)

Jorge   Period 2

Mozambique Macaws

4 birds

4 lbs. food $\underline{4\ birds}$

4 weeks   4 weeks = 1

1 bird ÷ 4 lbs. = .25 lbs. per bird per week

.25 lbs. × 12 weeks = 3 lbs. per bird

3 lbs. × 12 birds = 36 lbs. total

Total

        36 lbs.

        72 lbs.

    $\underline{+\ 48\ lbs.}$

    156 lbs. total

The bird keeper would need to buy 156 pounds of food to feed all three groups of birds.

1. Problem Statement:

   In this week's problem, the bird keeper at the zoo realizes that 2 crested cockatoos eat 2 pounds of bird seed every 2 weeks. He also saw that 3 Peruvian parrots eat 3 pounds of bird seed every 3 weeks, and that 4 Mozambique macaws eat 4 pounds of bird seed every 4 weeks. I'm supposed to find out how many pounds of bird seed 12 crested cockatoos, 12 Peruvian parrots, and 12 Mozambique macaws eat in 12 weeks.

2. Plan:

   To solve this problem I am first going to have to find out how many pounds of bird seed are needed for 12 birds of each kind. Then I'm going to have to multiply that amount of food for the 12 weeks for each kind of bird. Finally I will add all the subtotals together to get a grand total, which will tell me how much bird seed is needed. After that I should have my answer. The strategies I think I will use are multiplication and division with some addition at the end. I think that the keeper will need 72 pounds of food for the 12 crested cockatoos, 64 pounds of food for the 12 Peruvian parrots, and 56 pounds of food for the 12 Mozambique macaws, for a grand total of 192 pounds of bird seed.

3. Work:

   For this problem, I first read the problem and started working on converting the information on the 2 crested cockatoos to 12 crested cockatoos that needed food for 12 weeks. I found that 1 bird eats 1 pound of food every 2 weeks. I found this by dividing 2 birds by half (.5) to get 1 bird, then 2 pounds by half to get 1 pound. That means that 1 bird eats .5 pounds of food in a week. After that I took .5 pounds of food and multiplied it by 12 weeks. This gave me the amount of food 1 bird would eat in 12 weeks, which is 6 pounds. Finally I took 6 pounds of food and multiplied it by the 12 birds.

   For the Peruvian parrots I converted the information on the 3 parrots to 12 parrots, which was very similar to my approach on the first step of the problem even though the basic numbers had changed. I started by dividing 3 birds by 3 pounds to get 1 bird eating 1 pound of food every 3 weeks. Because 12 divided by 3 is 4, I knew that 1 bird ate 4 pounds of food in 12 weeks. Finally I took the 12 birds and multiplied it by 4 pounds to come up with my answer, 48.

(continues)

Figure 2.3 *(Continued)*	Secondary Problem-Solving Student Work Sample

For the third part of the problem I took all the information on the 4 Mozambique macaws and converted it for the 12 macaws. I first took the 4 birds and divided by 4 weeks to come up with 1 bird. Next I took the 1 bird and divided by the 4 pounds and saw that 1 bird eats .25 pounds of food every week. After that I took the .25 pounds of food and multiplied it by the 12 weeks, which told me that each bird eats 3 pounds of food every 12 weeks. Finally I took the 3 pounds of food and multiplied it by the 12 birds, which gave me my answer of 36 for this part of the problem.

For the last part of the problem I took the subtotals from all three types of birds and added them together to get the final total amount of food that the bird keeper would need to buy.

4. Answer:

I believe that the bird keeper will need to buy 156 pounds of bird seed: 72 pounds for the cockatoos, 48 pounds for the parrots, and 36 pounds for the macaws. I do not think that there could be another answer for this problem because I found out the relationships between 1 bird and the feeding schedule from the above information and based on that, my answer will not change because the ratios will stay the same for each type of bird and how much and how often it was fed for 12 weeks. If the bird keeper bought any more food he would have too much and if he bought any less he would have too little. I guessed that the cockatoos would eat 72 pounds of bird seed and they did, but when I guessed that the parrots would eat 64 pounds of food I was wrong because they actually ate 48 pounds of bird food, and when I guessed that the macaws would eat 56 pounds of food I was wrong because they actually ate 36 pounds of food. From this problem I learned that it is easy to be given information, but when you have to take that information and convert it for one bird over an amount of time it can be a lot more difficult and require more steps to the solution.

Suggested Problem-Solving Sequence for Secondary Students

Secondary students' success with problem solving depends on their foundational success with problem solving during the elementary school years. Students in middle school and high school need a strong understanding of mathematical concepts and vocabulary. If students lack successful experience with problem solving, they will likely be quite reticent about involving themselves in cooperative problem-solving activities. It is therefore essential to create the classroom conditions for students to experience success. This requires deliberate creation of a classroom atmosphere or culture in which students feel supported through the entire problem-solving process.

Peer support and interaction, self-reflection on performance, timely feedback, and the opportunity for revision are essential ingredients in the formula for student problem-solving success at the secondary level. Students who have received procedure-focused instruction in mathematics, as opposed to instruction for understanding of concepts, will find problem solving very frustrating. It is helpful to provide such students with multiple opportunities to explain their mathematical reasoning in writing before they are asked to do problem solving independently. Hearing other students' written explanations and seeing models of those written explanations are also very helpful.

Again, it is critical that students experience initial and continuing success with problem solving if they are to remain engaged and develop confidence in their mathematical reasoning ability. Teachers can deliberately promote this success by providing their students with regular opportunities to solve word problems and communicate their understanding in a structured way. We

> *If students lack successful experience with problem solving, they will likely be quite reticent about involving themselves in cooperative problem-solving activities.*

recommend the following sequence for introducing and developing the problem-solving process from the beginning to the end of the school year. Teachers in the middle school and high school grades should determine the appropriate pace for their individual classes.

1. Teacher and students solve the given problem together, creating a class Data Sheet and accompanying write-up. Repeat this process with a second Problem-Solving Task.

2. Students begin to work in small, cooperative groups to solve a new Problem-Solving Task.

3. In their groups, students create a Data Sheet (the mathematical work they did to solve the problem) and a write-up (the written explanation of their mathematical thinking and problem-solving process).

4. The whole class and teacher agree on the solution and complete a class write-up together.

5. Students compare their small-group write-ups to the whole class write-up and edit as needed so that they match.

6. Students next work in pairs to solve a new Problem-Solving Task, following the same process described in steps 3–5 above.

7. Students then attempt to complete the entire process independently, using the regular or alternative problem-solving methods (described later in this chapter). Provide teacher assistance as needed. Repeat this process one or two more times until the majority of students can complete a Data Sheet and accompanying write-up on their own.

8. Teacher and students design a problem-solving rubric (described later in this chapter) that will be used to evaluate student work and provide students with feedback on their independent

problem-solving performance. Include sufficient opportunities for student reflection and revision.

Differentiation

The entire problem-solving process described in this chapter is deliberately designed to support all students of different levels of skill and understanding; thus, this *is* differentiated instruction. However, in addition to the specific strategies suggested in Chapter 1 (many of which also apply to problem solving and are repeated in this section), we offer a few additional guidelines for meeting the learning needs of students at various levels of problem-solving ability.

Select problems that directly match current classroom instruction.

Begin the process with easier problems and fewer steps, so that students experience immediate success and develop a positive attitude toward the process.

Select problems that students can solve in various ways.

Select problems appropriate to students' instructional level and that can be extended or enriched for more able learners.

Teach and apply the problem-solving strategies to a variety of classroom applications and situations.

Provide vocabulary instruction and related support for all students; increase that support for English-language learners.

Post key mathematical vocabulary on a Math Word Wall.

Step 2: Problem Solving

Encourage the use of manipulatives and graphic representations.

Allow the use of calculators during problem-solving activities, emphasizing to students that the calculator is a tool to facilitate mathematical thinking while solving multiple-step problems.

Use the alternative method of problem solving described later in this chapter.

Model written explanation of mathematical reasoning on a regular basis.

Emphasize mathematical reasoning and evidence of that reasoning in the assessment process.

Have students add the word "because" after each step they write to extend their thinking and support their reasoning.

Provide effective peer interaction and support.

Encourage dialogue that emphasizes sense-making, particularly between students who understand the process and those who do not.

Include time for student self-reflection and revision of work.

Use flexible groups for students who are overly frustrated.

Find times during the day to offer one-on-one assistance to struggling students.

The Alternative Problem-Solving Method

One of the most effective ways to differentiate instruction and assist all students in developing their problem-solving skills is through the alternative problem-solving method developed by Jan Christinson. This method is introduced to students later in the school year, once they are thoroughly familiar with the problem-solving process described earlier in this chapter. The alternative problem-solving approach promotes greater peer interaction among students and provides more classroom support to help each student become an independent and confident problem solver.

The process is described in the following series of steps. For easy reference, a summary of the steps appears in a chart at the end of this section and as a template in the "Reproducibles" section at the end of this book.

1. *Select an appropriate problem.* Select a problem that matches the current unit of instruction. The problem should help students see the connection between what they are learning in the current math chapter or unit and its application to real life.

2. *Assign students to small cooperative groups.* Organize students into groups of three. (*Note:* The rotation process, described in steps 11 through 16, permits students to work with peers of differing abilities.)

3. *Distribute the problem and an alternative write-up guide.* Pass out the problem and an Alternative Problem-Solving Task Write-Up Guide to each student. Explain the three sections of the write-up guide and what students are to write in each of the sections.

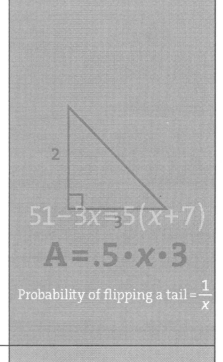

$$51-3x=5(x+7)$$
$$A=.5 \cdot x \cdot 3$$
Probability of flipping a tail $= \dfrac{1}{x}$

Step 2: Problem Solving

<table>
<tr><td colspan="2" align="center">Alternative Problem-Solving Task Write-Up Guide</td></tr>
<tr><td>Title of Problem</td><td>_____</td></tr>
<tr><td>Independent Work</td><td>(record what you did to try to solve the problem by yourself)</td></tr>
<tr><td>Cooperative Work</td><td>(record what you did to try to solve the problem with others.)</td></tr>
<tr><td>Answer and Verification</td><td>(write your answer and explain how you know your answer is correct mathematically)</td></tr>
</table>

4. *Have students count off.* Have students number themselves one, two, or three within each group. Each student then writes his or her assigned number on the top of a write-up guide. The student's number will be used for a rotation process.

5. *Have students create a Data Sheet.* Have each student prepare an individual Data Sheet on which students will record their own work (computation and/or graphic representation) as they attempt to solve the problem. They will record additional calculations as they continue working on it.

6. *Explain the "hint" process to students.* A hint can be a clarification of the information stated in the problem, a strategy, or even a mathematical formula. During the group problem-solving portion of this method, if students decide they have an insight into the mathematics necessary to solve the problem, they are invited to write that information or "hint" on the board. After the information is written on the board, the teacher has all the other students stop working so that the hint can be explained by the student(s) who wrote it. At this point, the cooperative

groups of three decide whether or not the hint gives useful information. Students then continue solving the problem.

During the hint process, the teacher should remain neutral about the information presented so that students have the opportunity to improve their own mathematical reasoning. This process helps students build self-confidence and develop a tenacious attitude toward mathematical problem solving.

7. *Let students attempt to solve the problem independently.* Give students five minutes to try to solve the problem independently. Whatever attempt they make to begin solving the problem should be recorded on their individual Data Sheets. During the five minutes, it is important that students *do not talk,* so that everyone gets a chance to try to solve the problem without any assistance. This part of the alternative problem-solving method also gives students an opportunity to consider what they might contribute when they start working with peers.

8. *Students record their independent work.* At the end of the allotted five minutes, have students prepare to write about their initial attempt to solve the problem. Ask them to write in complete sentences in the "Independent Work" section of the write-up guide. Those students who did not record anything on their Data Sheets can write their thoughts about the problem or any questions they have about the problem. Students must write, however, even if they only record that they read the problem and thought about it. This is an important step for students who are insecure about their math skills. It helps them to relax and feel more comfortable so that they will be receptive to the ideas soon to be shared by their team members.

9. *Begin initial group work.* At this point, have students work on solving the problem in their small groups of three for 10 to 12 minutes. Students record their group's work on their individual Data Sheets.

10. *Have students record the initial group work.* At the end of the allotted 10 to 12 minutes, students record what they did to solve the problem with the first group by writing a few sentences in the "Cooperative Work" section of the write-up guide.

11. *Do the first rotation.* After students have worked in the first cooperative group of three for 10 to 12 minutes, have the students numbered "1" in each group stand and rotate to another group, taking with them their Data Sheets and write-up guides. (*Note:* Students can rotate in a deliberate progression or randomly.)

12. *Begin work with the second group.* After the departure of one group member and the arrival of a new group member, students now work with the new group for another 10 to 12 minutes to continue solving the problem. The new group member shares with the other two students the cooperative work that was accomplished in that student's former group. The two other students share with the new member what they did in the first group work session. All three students add this new information to their own individual Data Sheets and continue working on the problem.

13. *Have students record the second group's new information.* Students now record a few more sentences about what they have done to solve the problem with the second group in the "Cooperative Work" section of the write-up guide.

Differentiation

14. *Do the second rotation.* Have the students numbered "2" in each group stand and take their Data Sheets and write-up guides to a new group. (Again, the rotations can occur in a deliberate progression or randomly.)

15. *Begin work with the third group.* Students add any new information from the former groups to their own Data Sheets in the same way described in #12. They then continue working with the new groups to solve the problem for another 10–12 minutes.

16. *Have students record the third group's new information.* Students now write a few sentences about their work with this third group in the "Cooperative Group" section of the write-up guide. (*Rotation note:* Try to rotate students at least twice so that they have the opportunity to work with three different groups. If time permits, students can rotate one more time so that all three students in the original groups have had a chance to move and change groups.)

17. *Ask students to complete the "Answer and Verification" section.* As students begin to think that they have solved the problem, they can start work on the third and final section of the write-up guide: the "Answer and Verification" section. Students use all the hints that were presented to the class and recorded on the board, along with the work they did in the three or more cooperative groups, to begin to develop their final solution and proof (verification) of that solution.

18. *Create the final product independently.* For homework, students use their Data Sheets and write-up guides to decide on their own solutions. Each student writes a summary on a separate piece of paper that contains a paragraph for each section of the write-up guide. (*Note:* For student populations that are not successful in completing and returning homework, the final-product step can be completed the next day in class.)

19. *Process the solution.* The next day, students return to class with their possible solutions. Have several students present their proposed solutions and verifications. As a class, discuss the actual correct solution and the mathematical concepts supporting that solution.

20. *Assess the completed student work.* Involve students in the peer- and self-assessment of their work, as described later in this chapter, before the teacher does any evaluation of student work.

Figure 2.4 is an example of a seventh-grade student's completed write-up guide using the alternative problem-solving method. (This is a sample Problem-Solving Task from the Math Forum @ Drexel, an excellent problem-solving resource for teachers. The Forum's "Problem of the Week" service [http://mathforum.org/pow/] provides challenging, nonroutine word problems for students to solve online in a mentored environment.)

The Teacher's Role in the Alternative Method

The role of the teacher during this highly engaging, interactive student process is to provide encouragement, support, and classroom management. Teacher instruction and explanation occur only after students have completed the "Answer and Verification" section and three written paragraphs. At that time, the teacher summarizes and points out the key mathematical concepts and skills that the students have been fully engaged in discovering during the group work and rotation steps.

MATH FORUM—PROBLEM OF THE WEEK

California Dreaming

As I watch the snow pile up outside, I'm dreaming of the sunny weather in California. Planning an imaginary trip across the country, from Allentown, PA, to Los Angeles, CA, will help keep me warm. I could use your help.

According to MapQuest [http://www.mapquest.com/], the total driving distance is 2,688.2 miles. With side trips and allowing for getting lost we will actually cover 2,800 miles. At times we will be on highways where we can travel from 50 to 70 miles per hour. At other times we will be on city streets with a speed limit of 35 miles per hour.

To help with our calculations, I'll provide the following:

- We will travel at 35 miles per hour for five hours of our trip.
- We will travel at 50 miles per hour for fourteen hours of our trip.
- We will travel at 65 miles per hour for fourteen hours of our trip.
- We will travel at 70 miles per hour for the remaining distance.

If we spend 8 hours a day driving, how many days will the trip take? How long will we drive on the last day?

Bonus: Following the MapQuest route, name the eleven states in order from Pennsylvania to California that you would travel through on this imaginary trip.

(continues)

Figure 2.4 *(Continued)*	**Completed Student Write-Up Guide (Alternative Problem-Solving Method Sample)**

Step 1. Find the remaining miles to travel.

35 mph x 5 hrs = 175 miles

50 mph x 14 hrs = 700 miles

65 mph x 14 hrs = 910 miles

175 + 700 + 910 = 1,785 miles

2,800 – 1,785 = 1,015 miles left to travel

$$\begin{array}{r} 35 \\ \times\, 5 \\ \hline 175 \end{array} \qquad \begin{array}{r} 50 \\ \times\, 14 \\ \hline 700 \end{array} \qquad \begin{array}{r} 65 \\ \times\, 14 \\ \hline 910 \end{array}$$

$$\begin{array}{r} 175 \\ 700 \\ +\,910 \\ \hline 1,785 \end{array} \qquad \begin{array}{r} 2,800 \\ -\,1,785 \\ \hline 1,015 \end{array}$$

Step 2. Find the total number of hours traveled.

1,015 miles ÷ 70 mph = 14.5 hours

5 + 14 + 14 + 14.5 = 47.5 total hours

$$\begin{array}{r} 14.5 \\ 70\,\overline{)1{,}015.0} \\ 70 \\ \hline 315 \\ 280 \\ \hline 350 \\ 350 \\ \hline 0 \end{array} \qquad \begin{array}{r} 5 \\ 14 \\ 14 \\ +\,14.5 \\ \hline 47.5 \end{array}$$

Step 3. Find the number of days traveled.

47.5 hours ÷ 8 hours per day = 5.9375 days

Since this is more than 5 full days, we need to travel 6 days.

$$\begin{array}{r} 5.9375 \\ 8\,\overline{)47.5} \\ 40 \\ \hline 75 \\ 72 \\ \hline 30 \\ 24 \\ \hline 60 \\ 56 \\ \hline 45 \\ 40 \\ \hline 5 \end{array}$$

Step 4. Find the amount of time traveled on the last day.

1 day = 8 hrs

5 days x 8 hours per day = 40 hours

47.5 – 40 = 7.5 hours traveled on the last day

Completed Student Write-Up Guide (Alternative Problem-Solving Method Sample)	Figure 2.4 *(Continued)*

PROBLEM-SOLVING WRITE-UP

Title of the Problem _California Dreaming_

1. **Individual Work** (Record what you did to try to solve the problem by yourself.)

   First, I wrote the main information on my worksheet. Second, I added up the hours traveled, 14 + 14 + 5, and got 33 hours. Then I divided 33 by 24, because there are 24 hrs in 1 day. I got 1 day and 9 hours, but this didn't help with the answer.

2. **Cooperative Work** (Record what you did to try to solve the problem with others.)

   Group #1: We divided 33 by 8 and got 4.125, but we didn't know what to do with this.

   Group #2: We tried to figure out how many hours of driving on the last day, but we didn't get much.

   Group #3: First, we multiplied to find the distances traveled: 35 mph x 5 hrs = 175 miles, 50 mph x 14 hrs = 700 miles, 65 mph x 14 hrs = 910 miles. Second, we subtracted: 2,688.2 miles – 175 – 700 – 910 = 903.2 miles. Then we divided 903.2 by 70 mph and got 12.90 more hours of driving. After that, we knew we had to figure out if we spent 8 hours a day driving, the trip would take 6 days. Last, we had to figure out how long we had to travel on the last day, but we didn't have time to finish.

3. **Answer and Verification** (Write your answer and explain how you know your answer is correct mathematically.) Use the back of the paper.

   My final answer is that we spent 6 days driving and it took 7.5 hours on the last day. How I found that was I multiplied (35 x 5) = 175, (50 x 14) = 700, (65 x 14) = 910. Then I added 175 + 700 + 910 and got 1,785 miles. I subtracted 1,785 miles from 2,800 total miles and got 1,015 miles. Next, I divided 1,015 miles by 70 mph and got 14.5. I added the hours: 5 + 14 + 14 + 14.5 and got 47.5. Then I divided 47.5 hours by 8 hours a day driving and got 5.9375. Because this is more than 5 days, the trip took 6 days. I wasn't done so I multiplied 5 x 8 and it equaled 40. I subtracted 47.5 - 40 and got 7.5 hours for how long it will take to drive on the last day.

(continues)

Figure 2.4 *(Continued)*	**Completed Student Write-Up Guide (Alternative Problem-Solving Method Sample)**

1-Page Summary – Problem Solving Write Up

First, I wrote the main information that was on my worksheet: 35 miles per hour for 5 hours of trip, 50 miles per hour for 14 hours of trip, 65 miles per hour for 14 hours of trip, and 70 miles per hour for remaining distance. The problem asked: "If we spend 8 hours a day driving, how many days will the trip take and how long will we drive on last day?" I added up the hours of the trip and got 33. Then I divided 33 by 24 hours in a day, but this didn't help me.

Later, with my first and second group, we tried to figure out the answer using 8 hours a day as the help calculation, but we didn't have much luck. My third group had better luck. We multiplied everything (35 x 5) = 175, (50 x 14) = 700, (65 x 14) = 910. Next, we had to find out the remaining number of miles. We found it by subtracting 2,688.2 – 1,785 = 903.2. Then we divided 903.2 by 70 mph and got 12.9 hours. We added this to the 33 hours and got 45.9. We divided that by 8 and got 5.73. We knew we had to get close to 45.9, so we added 8 five times. We didn't know what to do from there. We were lost, but knew it had to be somewhere around 6 days.

At home I was looking at my work I did in class. It didn't look right so I tried something else. My final answer and work is: We multiplied 35 mph x 5 = 175, then multiplied 50 mph x 14 and got 700, then multiplied 65 mph x 14 and got 910. Next, I added 910 + 700 + 175 and got 1,785. I knew it said in the problem that the total miles were 2,800, not 2,688.2, so I subtracted 2,800 – 1,785 and got 1,015 miles for the remaining distance. I wasn't done yet so I divided 1,015 by 70 mph, which was 14.5. After that I added the hours: 5 + 14 + 14 + 14.5 and got 47.5 hours of driving. Later I divided 47.5 hours by 8 hours a day which is 5.9375 days, so the trip took 6 days.

I wasn't finished yet. I needed to find out how long we drove on the last day. I knew we drove 8 hrs per day so I multiplied 8 x 5 whole days which equals 40 hours. I subtracted this from 47.5 hours and found that we drove 7.5 hours on the last day.

*Bonus: Pennsylvania, Ohio, Indiana, Illinois, Missouri, Kansas, Oklahoma, Texas, New Mexico, Arizona, California

Differentiation

However, to ensure problem-solving success for each and every student, teachers make themselves available for additional help to students before or after school and/or during lunch breaks. This outside-of-class assistance is especially important for struggling students *before* they attempt to complete the write-up independently. By providing that extra help when needed, teachers greatly assist students in becoming successful problem solvers.

The Time Factor

All of the steps of the alternate problem-solving method (with the exception of the independent work, which is deliberately designed for students to do independently after class) can be accomplished within a 54-minute class period. If the math period is only 42 minutes long, the teacher can simply choose to do one less rotation. Suggested time allotments for the initial independent student work and each of the rotations have been included in the preceding step descriptions and in the following summary of steps to give readers a sense of pacing. Although the recording of group work typically only takes about two to three minutes, the time allocated for students to record their group work in writing should be flexible and adjusted to the needs of the class.

Student Benefits

The alternative problem-solving method gives students an opportunity to attempt problem solving in a supportive environment. It provides peer interaction, mathematical information, and time to think and discuss. This powerful process builds student confidence with problem solving which, in turn, dramatically changes student attitudes toward mathematics!

The alternative problem-solving method gives students an opportunity to attempt problem solving in a supportive environment.

Step 2: Problem Solving

The Alternative Problem-Solving Method— A Summary of Steps

Preparation:

1. Select an appropriate problem.

2. Assign students to small cooperative groups of three.

3. Distribute the problem and an alternative write-up guide.

4. Have students count off (students number themselves one, two, or three within each group).

5. Have students create a Data Sheet.

6. Explain the "hint" process to students.

Solve the Problem:

7. Let students attempt to solve the problem independently (5 minutes).

8. Students record their independent work.

9. Begin initial group work (10–12 minutes).

10. Have students record the initial group work.

11. Do the first rotation (students numbered "1" rotate to new groups).

12. Begin work with the second group (10–12 minutes).

13. Have students record the second group's new information.

14. Do the second rotation (students numbered "2" rotate to new groups).

15. Begin work with the third group (10–12 minutes).

16. Have students record the third group's new information. (*Note:* The "hint" process introduced in #6 is ongoing during group work.)

17. Ask students to complete the "Answer and Verification" section.

18. Create the final product independently (homework).

19. Process the solution (next day in class).

20. Assess the completed student work (peer, self-, and teacher evaluations).

Formally Assessing Problem Solving

The first few Problem-Solving Tasks are done mainly to give students the experience of solving problems and to let them become familiar with the format for communicating their process and understanding. Teachers review students' initial work only to determine if they have followed directions and completed the process correctly. However, when students have successfully finished one or more Data Sheets and write-ups with their class-mates, and when they are able to complete a Problem-Solving Task independently, it is time to involve them in the assessment of their work. Assessment of problem solving begins with the design of a problem-solving rubric. In the following subsections, we describe in detail the steps we follow when involving students in both the design and use of a problem-solving rubric.

Creating a Problem-Solving Rubric

A *rubric* or *scoring guide* (these terms are used synonymously) is a set of performance criteria that enables both teachers and students to know the level or degree of proficiency reached on a particular piece of student work. We believe that all rubrics should use clearly understood, specific language descriptors upon which everyone (students, teachers, parents, and leaders) can agree, and that teachers should create rubrics in collaboration *with* students so that the rubrics will be truly understood *by* students. Many district and state assessments now include rubrics for evaluation of math tasks, but the criteria in them are highly subjective, such as in the example in Figure 2.5.

Figure 2.5	Sample of Typical Math Rubric

GENERALIZED MATH RUBRIC

4

- ❑ <u>Fully</u> accomplishes the purpose of the task
- ❑ Shows <u>full</u> grasp and use of the central mathematical idea
- ❑ Recorded work communicates thinking <u>clearly</u>, using <u>some</u> combination of written, symbolic, or visual means

3

- ❑ <u>Substantially</u> accomplishes the purpose of the task
- ❑ Shows <u>full</u> grasp and use of the central mathematical idea
- ❑ Recorded work <u>in large part</u> communicates thinking

2

- ❑ <u>Partially</u> accomplishes the purpose of the task
- ❑ Shows <u>partial but limited</u> grasp and use of the central mathematical idea
- ❑ Recorded work may be incomplete, misdirected, or not <u>clearly</u> presented

1

- ❑ <u>Little</u> or no progress toward accomplishing the purpose of the task
- ❑ Shows <u>little</u> or no grasp of the central mathematical idea
- ❑ Recorded work is <u>barely</u> (if at all) <u>comprehensible</u>

Note the subjective terminology underlined in the rubric in Figure 2.5. Teachers who attempted to score student papers using this rubric might find it challenging to agree with each other as to exactly what the underlined terms, such as "full" or "substantially," "in large part," or "partial but limited," actually mean. If reaching agreement proves challenging for professional educators, how much more difficult will it be for students to understand these terms?

The teacher-guided, student-generated rubric for mathematical problem solving is a special type of rubric. It must describe the essential criteria for acceptable performance in *specific, observable,* and *measurable* terms. It must produce fair and reliable evaluation of student write-ups. It must also be usable week after week—a generalized, yet still specific math problem-solving scoring guide with language descriptors that everyone understands.

Because it requires a sizeable block of instructional time to involve students in designing and revising assessment criteria, it is impractical to create a task-specific scoring guide for each Problem-Solving Task. In addition, teachers run the risk of "over-rubricizing"—a term we coined to mean involving students in the creation of too many rubrics and thus negating their enthusiasm for designing assessment criteria. Therefore, the problem-solving rubric must be thoughtfully crafted *once,* with an initial investment of time, so that it can be used throughout the rest of the year to evaluate student understanding on *every* Problem-Solving Task assigned.

How to Design the Problem-Solving Rubric

This is the sequence we follow with students each school year when it is time to begin evaluating problem-solving write-ups with a scoring guide.

1. *Decide on your performance levels.* We recommend using a four-level rubric or scoring guide, as opposed to ones that include five or six levels. The latter are often too vague or subtle in their wording of the criteria. Such rubrics make it difficult for both teachers and students to distinguish one level from another. An example of a four-level problem-solving rubric appropriate for use in secondary grades appears in Figure 2.6 (see pg. 69).

We recommend using a four-level rubric or scoring guide, as opposed to ones that include five or six levels. The latter are often too vague or subtle in their wording of the criteria.

2. *Choose a format.* When designing a problem-solving rubric, teachers can select either a holistic or an analytic format. *Analytic* rubrics represent all the criteria for each performance level in a chart format. Each of the problem-solving components (i.e., Data Sheet, math process, math vocabulary, write-up guide directions, and so on) is represented by specific criteria for *each level* of the rubric. The benefit of a properly designed analytic rubric is that it provides very specific diagnostic information for teachers, showing where students are scoring well and in which areas they need to improve.

Holistic rubrics simply list all the criteria for a particular level beneath that level label. Holistic rubrics are often easier for students to use because they appear less complex, and list all requirements under one heading; nevertheless, this type of rubric still provides teachers with the important information they need regarding students' mathematical understanding and process. We recommend using a holistic format.

3. *Consider the problem-solving elements.* Teachers next consider the following list of problem-solving elements before they begin creating the rubric with their students. As you consider each of these elements, decide where you would place each one in the performance levels you have selected, and how you would describe it for that level. This is an excellent activity to do in grade-level or math department teams before each teacher leads his or her class through the creation of a problem-solving rubric with student input.

- Right answer
- Wrong answer, right process
- Clarity of written explanation

- Mathematical reasoning

- Proof or verification of answer

- Simple calculation errors

- Inclusion of appropriate math vocabulary

- Following write-up guide directions

4. *Refer to the Problem-Solving Task Write-Up Guide and practice problems to create rubric criteria.* When students and teachers first begin authoring the rubric, they look at the Problem-Solving Task Write-Up Guide and the practice problems displayed around the room to help them think of criteria to include. The Problem-Solving Guide focuses student attention on the important need to match the rubric to the write-up directions. The posters students created provide powerful examples of mathematical reasoning, the use of math vocabulary, the process the students went through to arrive at the solution, and to what degree the written work communicated mathematical understanding. These examples help students think about both quantity and quality criteria to include in the rubric. It is important to remember that the criteria included in the problem-solving rubric should emphasize the *mathematics* students are to communicate in their written work.

5. *Start with "Proficient."* Student problem-solving work that is to be formally assessed should provide evidence of proficiency. For this reason, most teachers and students write the criteria for the "Proficient" level of the rubric first. However, before they can do this effectively, they need to discuss what *proficient* means. Write down suggested synonyms or phrases that convey what proficiency means. (*Note:* This term may carry different connotations depending on your own particular state's context.

Proficiency should *not* be regarded as a minimum, average, or basic level of competency. It indicates a level of student performance between average and exemplary or advanced.) Discuss with colleagues, reach an agreement, and then write the *specific, observable, measurable criteria* that demonstrate problem-solving proficiency in the appropriate section of the problem-solving rubric.

6. *Next, write the "Exemplary" criteria.* Refer to the criteria for proficiency and then decide what an exemplary problem-solving Data Sheet and write-up should look like. Write specific, observable, measurable criteria *in relation to the "Proficient" criteria.* This level of the scoring guide should provide students with challenging criteria that will enable them to go above and beyond the expectations for proficiency and demonstrate advanced work.

7. *Next, write the "Progressing" and "Beginning" criteria.* We have streamlined and simplified the problem-solving rubric for these two remaining levels to keep the focus on proficiency and above. If students understand that the goal is proficiency and higher, as defined by the rubric criteria, it makes sense to describe the progressing and beginning levels in relation to proficiency. When students know that they can revise their work to meet any unmet criteria in the "Proficient" category, it becomes much easier for them to evaluate performance in relation to that designated goal.

Figure 2.6 shows a problem-solving rubric that middle school and high school math teachers and students can use as a guide to design their own. Once the problem-solving rubric is finalized, it can be used to evaluate every Problem-Solving Task, regardless of the particular math strand or standards in focus.

Sample Problem-Solving Scoring Guide (Secondary Grades)	Figure 2.6

Name _____ Title of Problem _____

PROBLEM-SOLVING SCORING GUIDE: MIDDLE SCHOOL AND HIGH SCHOOL

Exemplary:
- ❑ All "Proficient" criteria *plus*:
- ❑ Verifies answer mathematically
- ❑ Written work explains verification of answer

Proficient:
- ❑ Correct answer
- ❑ Solves problem on Data Sheet using computation and/or graphic representation
- ❑ Written explanation matches Data Sheet
- ❑ Shows correct mathematical reasoning
- ❑ Uses math vocabulary appropriate to problem
- ❑ Follows all Problem-Solving Guide directions to complete write-up

Progressing:
- ❑ Meets 4–5 of the "Proficient" criteria

Beginning:
- ❑ Meets fewer than 4 of the "Proficient" criteria
- ❑ Task to be repeated after remediation

Peer's Evaluation _____

I think the score is a _____ because _____

Self-Evaluation _____

I think my score is a _____ because _____

Teacher's Evaluation _____ because _____

_____

Note: Proficiency must address the *mathematics.*

Students have ongoing opportunities to reflect upon and revise their work with feedback from the scoring guide.

Here are a few of the benefits of using a simpler problem-solving rubric that emphasizes demonstration of proficiency:

The focus is kept on the proficient and exemplary levels, not on the lower levels of student performance.

The "Progressing" and "Beginning" criteria often emphasize the negative—what students are not able to do or what their work is lacking. When written as "meets 4–5 of the 'Proficient' criteria," they are phrased as positives.

Writing criteria for the lower two categories is often problematic. Students may meet or demonstrate certain criteria but not others. Again, when written as shown in the model, this problem is eliminated.

Student papers can be scored much more quickly when performance is measured by fewer—but more important—criteria representing proficiency.

A Feedback Tool for Revision

Feedback from the rubric should focus student attention on which criteria for proficiency have already been met and which are yet to be attained. To do this, we often check off the criteria that have been met and highlight those that have not. This simple process gives students immediate feedback. Also, the teacher can ask the student whether the highlighted criteria represent something the student does not know, or whether those items simply were overlooked. As soon as the student revises the work to meet those particular criteria, the teacher can check them off. When the rubric is used in this way, the student recognizes that it is a feedback tool to aid revision and improve student performance.

Weighting and Grading Issues

Whenever educators consider using rubrics to evaluate student work, the subject of grading always arises. For the problem-solving rubric, there is the question of how to weight the criteria in the "Proficient" category. Is each of these criteria equal in terms of mathematical importance and therefore deserving of the same number of points? For example, a student follows the Problem-Solving Guide directions but does not include correct mathematical reasoning. Isn't the latter more important? Doesn't it therefore deserve greater weight (in terms of points) when determining the overall score?

One way to resolve this is to announce to students that to achieve and demonstrate proficiency on the final evaluation of their work, *all* criteria for "Proficient" must be met. Student work that does not meet all criteria is scored as being either "Progressing" or "Beginning." If students have had the rubric from the beginning of their work on the Problem-Solving Task, this is a fair expectation. It also prevents imprecise averaging of criteria to determine a grade, which often occurs when no clearly defined demonstrations of proficiency have been established beforehand with students.

The topic of assigning letter grades to rubric-scored evaluations of student performance is deep and complex. Our position is that formative work should not be graded. Only summative work should receive a grade. Readers interested in this topic should refer to four outstanding works on this subject: Robert Marzano, *Transforming Classroom Grading* (2000); Thomas Guskey and Jane Bailey, *Developing Grading and Reporting Systems for Student Learning* (2001); Ken O'Connor, *How to Grade for Learning: Linking Grades to Standards, Second Edition* (2002); and Douglas B. Reeves, "The Case Against the Zero" (2004).

The topic of assigning letter grades to rubric-scored evaluations of student performance is deep and complex. Our position is that formative work should not be graded.

Using the Rubric to Assess

Teachers who choose to further involve their students in the assessment of their problem-solving work may wish to show them how to evaluate their work and the work of their peers using the rubric they helped create. Our book, *Student Generated Rubrics: An Assessment Model to Help All Students Succeed* (1998) fully describes the procedure for involving students in designing scoring guides and then teaching them how to self- and peer-assess their work.

We recommend giving students more than one opportunity to demonstrate proficiency on a Problem-Solving Task. The scoring guide is a tool for helping students understand and reach proficiency. We all know that, for many students, proficiency does not occur the first time around. Teachers need to decide for themselves to what extent students can use the scoring-guide feedback to revise their work before moving on to a new task.

The best way to explain quality is by showing examples of it. It is important to provide students with exemplars or models of both proficient and exemplary work. This is an essential part of helping students make the connection between *written* descriptions of quality and proficiency and *visible demonstrations* of quality and proficiency specific to the problem-solving write-up requirements.

Benefits of the Problem-Solving and Rubric Assessment Process

Secondary teachers who make the problem-solving and rubric assessment processes a regular part of the balanced math program will see many benefits. Students who consistently and regularly engage in structured problem-solving activities will find themselves

Reader's Assignment

better prepared to reason mathematically and to think logically. They will be able to apply their problem-solving skills successfully, not only in the math classroom and on standardized test measures, but also in the authentic math situations they will encounter throughout life.

Reader's Assignment

Begin designing your problem-solving component based on the information presented in this chapter.

First, select a problem according to the guiding questions for selecting worthwhile problems. Solve that problem as recommended and write up your process using the write-up guide template. Finally, design the first draft of a problem-solving rubric to assess your own students' problem solving.

Refer to the sample Problem-Solving Task Write-Up Guide template in the "Reproducibles" section at the end of this book and the grade-specific problem-solving information presented in Chapters 6, 7, and 8. Refer also to Chapter 9 for answers to frequently asked questions regarding step 2, Problem Solving.

Step 3: Conceptual Understanding

Essential Questions

What is conceptual understanding? Why is it important in mathematics?

How is conceptual understanding different from procedural understanding?

Definitions

Consider these two definitions from mathematics researcher and author, John Van De Walle (2004, p. 27), and then determine how they match or extend your own.

> *Conceptual knowledge of mathematics consists of logical relationships constructed internally and existing in the mind as a network of ideas . . . . By its very nature, conceptual knowledge is knowledge that is understood.*

> *Procedural knowledge of mathematics is knowledge of the rules and the procedures that one uses in carrying out routine mathematical tasks and also the symbolism that is used to represent mathematics.*

Rationale

Educators deserve to know the "why" of a new process before they are expected to engage in the "how" of it. The following four passages thoughtfully address persuasive reasons for designing and teaching a conceptual unit of mathematics:

> *If we want students to know what mathematics is, as a subject, they must understand it. Knowing mathematics, really knowing it, means understanding it. When we memorize rules for moving symbols around on a paper we may be learning something, but we are not learning mathematics.*

> *When we memorize names and dates we are not learning history; when we memorize titles of books and authors we are not learning literature. Knowing a subject means getting inside it and seeing how things work, how things are related to each other, and why they work like they do (Hiebert, 1997, p. 2).*

> *Investigations have consistently shown that an emphasis on teaching for meaning has positive effects on student learning, including better initial learning, greater retention, and increased likelihood that the ideas will be used in new situations. These results have also been found in studies conducted in high-poverty areas (Cawelti, 1999, p. 120).*

> *If students don't understand the concepts, then it's likely that they're going to forget, and the teachers are going to have to go back and review and review (Hiebert, 2003, p. 24).*

The Conceptual Understanding Unit of Study

Designing a conceptual unit of mathematical study is an effective way for teachers to counteract the conventional practice of relying on the math textbook to dictate what to teach and how to assess learning. Developing a conceptual unit enables teachers to examine the standards and decide what is truly essential for student success (often referred to as *Power Standards*—described in Chapter 5) and then use those identified essentials to focus their day-to-day planning of instruction, learning activities, and assessment. A conceptual approach to learning mathematics helps students develop depth of mathematical understanding by connecting meaning to procedures.

Without the understanding that comes from meaning-based instruction, students do not retain information. An example of this is the topic of adding fractions with unlike denominators. For students to be successful with this concept, they must understand the ideas of part-whole relationship, adding similar-size pieces, and equivalency. Without this conceptual understanding, they are left to memorize a set of procedural steps that do not make any sense to them.

Developing students' conceptual understanding is at the heart of effective mathematics instruction. Step 3 of a balanced math program is designed to help teachers, whether working alone or collaboratively, prepare a conceptual unit aimed at deepening student understanding of that unit's central mathematical focus.

> *A conceptual approach to learning mathematics helps students develop depth of mathematical understanding by connecting meaning to procedures.*

Designing a Conceptual Unit

The conceptual understanding step is the portion of the math period during which students engage in a lesson or activity as part of a focused mathematics unit of study that lasts from two to four weeks. The Conceptual Understanding Unit lesson and related learning activities take place at the conclusion of Math Review and Mental Math, and require approximately 35 minutes of an hour-long math period. When the total instructional period is less than an hour (say, 42 to 54 minutes), the length of the conceptual unit lesson is adjusted accordingly.

Here is an overview of the 20-step sequence we follow when designing, teaching, and assessing a conceptual unit. This sequence and the particular terms used in it are described in detail in later sections.

1. *Establish the central mathematical focus for the unit—* a particular topic that students need to learn in depth. For example, a unit focus could be fractions, or it might be multiplication and division of decimals, two- and three-dimensional shapes, and so on.

2. *Locate the grade-specific math standards* addressing that particular topic.

3. *"Unwrap" those identified standards* to determine the *concepts* (what students need to know) and the *skills* (what students need to be able to do).

4. *Determine the essential mathematical concepts* using the knowledge package process (described later in this chapter).

5. *Decide on the Big Ideas* (the important understandings students are to discover *on their own* by the end of the unit).

6. *Write the Essential Questions* that will focus both instruction and assessment and lead students to discover the Big Ideas.

7. *Design an end-of-unit post-assessment* closely aligned to the "unwrapped" concepts, skills, and Big Ideas.

8. *Create a rubric or scoring guide* to evaluate the post-assessment.

9. *Design a pre-assessment* aligned to the end-of-unit post-assessment and an accompanying scoring guide.

10. *Plan the instructional lessons* and activities for the unit, guided by the Essential Questions.

11. *Share the Essential Questions* for the unit with students and post the questions visibly in the classroom.

12. *Administer the pre-assessment* to students.

13. *Score the pre-assessments* using the accompanying scoring guide and analyze the results to differentiate instruction.

14. *Begin teaching the unit* according to the planned instructional lessons and activities.

15. *Assess student understanding* informally throughout the unit, using assessment results to make appropriate changes in instruction.

16. *Share with students* the post-assessment scoring guide and then administer the assessment.

17. *Peer-, self-, and teacher-assess* the completed post-assessment using the accompanying scoring guide.

18. *Ask students to write a self-reflection* about their learning in relation to their assessment results.

Step 3: Conceptual Understanding

Writing curriculum and designing units of study is time-intensive work, best accomplished in collaboration with one or more grade-level, course, or department colleagues.

19. *Create individual student folders* for the collection of important student work products, including formative assessments and the end-of-unit post-assessment.

20. *Spend a few moments* engaged in your own self-reflection.

The Value of Planning a Unit Collaboratively

Writing curriculum and designing units of study is time-intensive work, best accomplished in collaboration with one or more grade-level, course, or department colleagues. Whether done before the start of a new school year, or completed during the year as needed, it takes time to think deeply about the essential mathematical understandings we want students to develop. Nevertheless, this investment of time yields one of the classroom teacher's best returns: planned instruction and assessment that lead to greater student understanding.

In many respects, teaching is still an isolated profession. Teachers rarely receive the valuable opportunity to collaborate with colleagues. Whatever instructional planning they do is usually done alone and on their own time—even though we know the power of two or more teachers gathered together to plan cooperatively. We see this collaboration as a critical need for schools and districts that are serious about implementing instructional change.

Teachers belong at the center of all instructional decisions. When encouraged to use their experience and knowledge of subject matter to develop curricular focus, they create powerful learning experiences for students.

Here, then, are the details of the 20 steps to designing, teaching, and assessing a conceptual unit of understanding in mathematics. A conceptual unit design template that can be duplicated for instructional use appears in the "Reproducibles" section at the end of this book.

1. *Establish the central mathematical focus for the unit —a particular topic that students need to learn in depth.* Working with your grade-level, course, or department colleague(s), identify a particular concept that students typically struggle with, one that requires more time and hands-on learning activities than usual for students to really understand it. For secondary-grade students, such topics might include: linear equations; adding and subtracting fractions with unlike denominators; area, perimeter, and volume; and fraction-decimal-percentage equivalency, to name but a few. This identified topic will become the focus of the unit you will design and teach conceptually.

2. *Locate the grade- or course-specific math standards addressing that particular topic.* Refer to the district or state math standards for your grade level or course and find the specific standards or indicators that match the mathematical focus you have selected for your unit.

3. *"Unwrap" those identified standards to determine the* concepts *(what students need to know) and the* skills *(what students need to be able to do).* To "unwrap" standards, first read carefully the wording of each standard you have identified. Underline the important *concepts* (nouns or noun phrases) and circle the *skills* (verbs) related to those concepts. Then, represent those concepts and skills on a graphic organizer of choice (a bulleted list, outline, or concept map). Although examples of more challenging "unwrapped" math concepts and skills appear later in this chapter and in Chapters 6, 7, and 8, here is a simple example of an "unwrapped" math standard for

the conceptual unit topic of estimation. Note that the skill "applies" has been capitalized rather than circled:

> **Estimation standard:** The student APPLIES numerical estimation with whole numbers up to 999, simple fractions, and money.
>
> Concepts:
>
> Estimation
>
> - Numerical estimation
> - Whole numbers to 999
> - Simple fractions
> - Money
>
> Skills:
>
> - APPLIES (estimation with whole numbers, fractions, money)

Source: Ainsworth, 2003a.

4. *Determine the essential mathematical concepts using the knowledge package process.* The knowledge package method, described near the end of this chapter, is another way in which teachers can find the essential mathematics within a standard. Please refer to the section entitled "The Knowledge Package Process" for details.

5. *Decide on the Big Ideas (the important understandings students are to discover* on their own *by the end of the unit).* In planning a conceptual unit together, grade-level colleagues ask, "What two or three essential mathematical understandings [Big Ideas] do we want the students to discover *on their own* by the time they complete this unit of study?" This question and the ensuing discussion to determine the essential focus of the unit are extremely important. They help the participating

teachers clarify, in advance of instruction, the main ideas students need to understand or important conclusions students need to draw about the standard(s) the teachers are preparing to teach. Here are two suggested Big Ideas relating to the "unwrapped" concepts and skills in the preceding estimation-standard example:

Estimation comes close to an exact number.

Whether you need to estimate or find the exact answer depends on the particular situation.

6. ***Write the Essential Questions that will focus both instruction and assessment and lead students to discover the Big Ideas.*** Teachers next write Essential Questions to share with students at the beginning of the unit, to interest them in the topic. These guiding questions—matched to the Big Ideas—forecast the learning goals for the unit of study. Their purpose is to help students make insightful connections about the "unwrapped" math concepts and skills they are learning. Students will eventually respond to these Essential Questions with the Big Ideas stated in their own words.

However, the Essential Questions for a conceptual unit do much more than inform students about what they are going to learn. They serve as an *instructional filter* for teachers to use when deciding which lessons and activities are necessary to develop student understanding of the unit's key focus. They enable teachers to determine if the math textbook program is sufficient to teach the particular "unwrapped" concepts and skills, or whether teachers need to search out supplemental materials that are more closely matched to their instructional needs. If other resources do indeed have to be explored, teachers again apply the filter of the Essential Questions to select the most appropriate instructional materials. In this way, the teacher is making these important decisions rather than relying on the textbook to do so.

Here is a sample pair of Essential Questions for the estimation standard:

> *What is estimation?*
> (Estimation comes close to an exact number.)
>
> *When and how do we use it?*
> (Whether you need to estimate or find the exact answer depends on the particular situation.)

Note the corresponding Big Ideas in parentheses. The first Big Idea is a desired student response to the first Essential Question: the student should be able to provide a definition of *estimation*. The second Essential Question and corresponding Big Idea response represent a higher level of thinking; that is, students must make a broader connection and demonstrate their understanding of the concept of estimation in an applied way.

7. *Design an end-of-unit post-assessment closely aligned to the "unwrapped" concepts, skills, and Big Ideas.* As soon as the "unwrapped" concepts, skills, and Big Ideas have been determined, teachers next design a suitable *post-assessment* to administer at the end of the unit. A suitable post-assessment meets two essential criteria. First, it directly aligns with the "unwrapped" concepts, skills, Big Ideas, and Essential Questions that were used to establish the foundation for the unit. Second, it provides students with the opportunity to demonstrate their full range of understanding of the "unwrapped" concepts and skills and allows them to respond to the Essential Questions with Big-Idea responses stated in their own words.

To meet these two requirements, teachers often design a performance-based assessment *and* a more traditional type of math assessment. With more than one type of assessment, students have the opportunity to demonstrate their understanding in multiple ways. The first assessment type—usually a Problem-Solving Task, as described in Chapter 2—allows students to show to what extent they can apply the math concepts and skills they learned during the unit to a problem-solving situation. In addition, teachers can ask students to say or write their Big-Idea responses to the Essential Questions. The second type—a more traditional assessment—requires students to solve computation problems matched to the focus of the unit. Teachers review available assessment resources (the math series in use, supplemental materials, and so on) to select assessment items that match their purpose. If they cannot find an appropriate assessment in published materials, they simply create their own.

The end-of-unit post-assessment does not replace the informal assessments *for* learning that teachers routinely conduct on a daily basis. Teachers use the results of ongoing informal assessments to differentiate instruction. This includes providing struggling students with additional assistance or intervention and advanced students with enrichment or acceleration *before* they take the end-of-unit post-assessment. An example of a secondary-grade assessment that contains a performance-based task is provided later in this chapter.

8. *Create a rubric or scoring guide to evaluate the post-assessment.* For the traditional assessment, the participating teachers can simply score the student papers as they are

> *With more than one type of assessment, students have the opportunity to demonstrate their understanding in multiple ways.*

accustomed to doing. However, they will, more than likely, need a rubric or scoring guide to evaluate the performance-based portion of the assessment. Establishing clear-cut criteria *in advance* will help students better understand the assessment directions and will enable them to set personal goals for their learning.

To design a scoring guide with the customary four performance levels, refer back to the assessment itself. Identify the specific elements the students are to include in their written work. Then, write *specific* descriptors that will let students know exactly what they have to do to demonstrate proficiency on the assessment. After that, write the specific descriptors for the other performance levels. (For additional guidelines, please refer again to the section on writing a math rubric with students in Chapter 2.)

9. *Design a pre-assessment aligned to the end-of-unit post-assessment and an accompanying scoring guide.* Before beginning any instructional planning for the conceptual unit, teachers design a pre-assessment matched to the format and items of the post-assessment. Usually they can use the same rubric that they developed for the post-assessment to evaluate the pre-assessment student papers (as long as the assessments are the same or similar).

10. *Plan the instructional lessons and activities for the unit, guided by the Essential Questions.* With grade-level, course, or department colleagues, teachers now review their math series and any supplemental materials through the lens of their Essential Questions and decide on the specific instructional

activities that will advance student understanding of the unit focus. This filtering process promotes the alignment of curriculum, instruction, and assessment. All lessons and activities presented during the course of the unit should prepare students for success on the post-assessment(s).

If a particular lesson or activity matches the Essential Questions, great! If it does not align, determine whether it can be modified so that it does. If it cannot be modified, continue searching resources for lessons or activities that can be.

11. *Share the Essential Questions for the unit with students and post the questions visibly in the classroom.* To set the stage for the upcoming unit, the teacher displays the Essential Questions in the classroom and lets students know that by the end of the unit, they will need to be able to respond to each of those questions. The teacher then asks students to give initial responses to the questions. This enables students to begin thinking about the topic of the unit and gives the teacher insights as to what students may already know about this subject.

12. *Administer the pre-assessment to students.* Teachers next let students know that they need students to complete a pre-assessment, to help the teachers plan their instruction. Tell students that the pre-assessment will be very similar to what they will see on the post-assessment at the end of the unit. Ask students to do their best, but remind them not to worry if they do not know the answers, because they have not yet been taught this information. Then, administer the pre-assessment to the students.

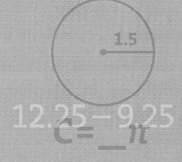

The median of: 1, 2, 3, 4, 5

Step 3: Conceptual Understanding

Remember to incorporate into Math Review and Mental Math the computational skills that relate to the conceptual understanding of the topic the students are studying.

13. *Score the pre-assessments using the accompanying scoring guide and analyze the results to differentiate instruction.* The chief benefit of giving a pre-assessment is that it enables teachers to find out, before any instruction takes place, which students are already proficient and need enrichment or acceleration, which students are almost proficient, and which students are far from proficient and will likely need intervention. These assessment results will greatly assist teachers in differentiating instruction for all their students as part of their unit planning.

14. *Begin teaching the unit according to the planned instructional lessons and activities.* We believe that students need the opportunity to wrestle with mathematical ideas to construct personal meaning. Here, *depth of student understanding* is the teacher's goal. To achieve this, present the selected activities and lessons as often as possible in a hands-on manner to help students build their own understanding of the "unwrapped" concepts and skills. Remember to incorporate into Math Review and Mental Math the computational skills that relate to the conceptual understanding of the topic the students are studying.

Students complete the conceptual lessons and activities individually, in pairs, cooperatively in teams, and/or together as a class. Often we evaluate these formative activities only for completion and demonstration of students' current level of understanding, using this feedback to modify and improve our instruction.

15. *Assess student understanding informally throughout the unit, using assessment results to make appropriate changes in instruction.* More and more, teachers are realizing the

value of conducting informal assessments *for* learning. These assessments are formative, shorter in length and duration than more formal evaluations, and provide timely feedback to both students and teacher. Students use the results from such ongoing assessments to reflect on their performance, measure their progress toward attainment of their personal learning goals, and make a plan for improvement. Teachers use the results from these "check-in" assessments to monitor and adjust instruction to meet the varying needs of all students.

16. *Share with students the post-assessment scoring guide and then administer the assessment.* When all instruction and learning activities for the conceptual unit have been completed, inform the students that it is time for the end-of-unit assessment. Distribute the scoring guide that will be used to evaluate the student responses on the performance portion of the assessment, explain the criteria, and encourage students to refer to the scoring guide for guidance as they complete their post-assessments.

17. *Peer-, self-, and teacher-assess the completed post-assessment using the accompanying scoring guide.* Secondary students typically assess the work of their peers and then compare those evaluations with their own self-assessment of performance. Teachers complete the final evaluation of students' end-of-unit assessments.

As described in step 2, teaching students how to assess their own work and the work of their peers increases individual student understanding of the evaluation process. By seeing a variety of work samples, secondary students come to understand that there are different levels of work quality. Presenting students with various models of proficient and exemplary work helps them to produce that level of quality themselves.

18. **Ask students to write a self-reflection about their learning in relation to their assessment results.** After returning the evaluated post-assessments to students, ask students to respond to three self-reflection questions:

    - *What did I learn well during this unit?*

    - *What do I still need to work on?*

    - *What is my plan to improve?*

    These questions help students to determine to what degree they learned the concepts, skills, and Big Ideas of the unit and to identify specific areas in which they need to improve. It is important to ask students to write a sentence or two setting out their specific plan for improvement during the next math unit, so that they take ownership of their own learning process.

19. **Create individual student folders for the collection of important student work products, including formative assessments and the end-of-unit post-assessment.** This is an organizational and management step that can occur whenever teachers wish. A folder or other organized collection of key student work products and assessments is a practical way to keep track of all completed unit papers. Teachers do this by placing the selected student papers in construction-paper folders or index file folders marked with individual student names. These folders may also include any Problem-Solving Task write-ups related to the conceptual unit focus.

    Students can take part in this process by labeling the cover of the folder with their names, title of the math unit, and any other identifying information required. On the inside cover, list the four criteria that the teacher will use to grade the folder:

- Neat
- Complete
- On time
- Organized

A student's completed unit folder can be sent home for parent review and comments before the teacher places it into the mathematics portfolio. The portfolio is an ongoing collection of the year's math conceptual unit folders that is reviewed during parent conferences and at other times during the school year. Teachers may also copy and forward representative samples of student learning to the student's next math teacher. The unit folders in the portfolio are given to the student at the end of the semester, course, or academic year.

20. *Spend a few moments engaged in your own self-reflection.* With the conceptual unit now completed, teachers can use the following four questions to reflect on the success of the unit:

- *What went well in the design and implementation of this unit? What did not?*
- *What insights into student learning did the pre- and post-assessments yield?*
- *What changes or improvements do I want to make when I teach this unit the next time?*
- *What changes or improvements do I want to make when designing my next unit?*

> *The portfolio is an ongoing collection of the year's math conceptual unit folders that is reviewed during parent conferences and at other times during the school year.*

Secondary Example of Conceptual Unit Planning

States now include standards for algebra in every grade and provide grade-specific learning expectations (indicators) to meet those standards. Because algebra is a widely recognized area of need in terms of student performance on state mathematics assessments, we selected this topic to illustrate the foundational design of a secondary-grade conceptual unit.

Here are the key components of an eighth-grade conceptual unit to address the topic of algebra:

The "unwrapped" standards, with accompanying Big Ideas and Essential Questions

The performance-based, end-of-unit post-assessment

The matching rubric or scoring guide to evaluate student proficiency

Once this foundation for the unit is established, grade 8 (or grade 9) teachers can use it as a guide to select appropriate lessons and hands-on learning activities from their particular textbook series and supplemental instructional materials. A planning template for designing a complete conceptual unit appears in the "Reproducibles" section at the end of this book. Figure 3.1 shows an example of a completed conceptual unit design. In addition, readers will find a conceptual unit appropriate for grade 6, grades 7–8, and grades 9–10 students in Chapters 6, 7, and 8, respectively. Chapter 9 sets out a weekly teaching schedule that includes a conceptual unit and the other components of our balanced math program model.

Secondary Example of Conceptual Unit Planning

Figure 3.1   Sample Completed Conceptual Unit Design

Grade: 8

Conceptual Unit Focus: Algebra

Standards and Indicators Matched to Unit Focus: [Here teachers list and "unwrap" the full text of the relevant standard and indicators from individual district or state documents for the selected topic. For this example, we used Standard 4: Graphing Linear Equations and Inequalities, from the state of Indiana. Note the use of a two-column chart. The "unwrapped"-skills column appears next to the "unwrapped"-concepts column. Each identified skill is matched to the concept next to it, such as "*graph* linear equations," "*write* equation of a line," and so on.]

"Unwrapped" Concepts and Skills:

Concepts	Skills
Students need to know about:	Students need to be able to do:
1. Linear equation	**1.** Graph
2. Slope, *x*-intercept, and *y*-intercept	**2.** Find (given two points, an equation, or graph)
3. Slope-intercept form	**3.** Write (equation); Understand (relationship of *y*-intercept and slope)
4. Equation of a line	**4.** Write
5. Equation of a line given data points—slope of a line	**5.** Write and make predictions; Describe in terms of the data
6. Linear inequalities in two variables	**6.** Graph

Topics or Context (resources used to teach the "unwrapped" concepts and skills):

❑ Graphing lines on the floor

❑ Scatter plots with height-distance traveling

❑ Roller-coaster activity

Big Ideas:

1. A linear equation describes a line with given points and a slope. Linear equations can be used to describe data.

2. The point-slope formula can be used to find linear equations.

3. Lines can have negative and positive slopes.

Essential Questions:

1. What is a linear equation, and how is it used?

2. What is the point-slope formula, and how is it used?

3. What is important to know about lines and slopes?

End-of-Unit Assessment: "Ride the Wild Side"

Sketch and design a roller coaster on one piece of paper. Your design must include eight hills of various slopes. Write the equations used to determine each slope on a separate paper. Then design a poster or physical model of your roller coaster. Write about the exciting features of your roller coaster.

(continues)

Figure 3.1 *(Continued)*	Sample Completed Conceptual Unit Design

Scoring Guide:

Exemplary:

❑ All "Proficient" criteria met *plus*:

❑ More than eight hills included, with correct equations and slopes

Proficient:

❑ Roller coaster is complete and connected—a workable design

❑ Eight hills are included in roller coaster

❑ Equations for eight slopes of the hills are correct

❑ Slopes of hills are correctly calculated

❑ Roller-coaster poster or physical model matches slope calculations

❑ Written features of roller coaster are included

Progressing:

❑ Meets 4–5 of the "Proficient" criteria

Beginning:

❑ Meets fewer than 4 of the "Proficient" criteria

❑ Assessment task to be repeated after remediation

Peer's Evaluation (Optional)

_____

Self-Evaluation

_____

Teacher's Evaluation

_____

Source: Adapted from work by Cinda Davis, Gary Emmert, and Patrick Ward, MSD of Wayne Township, IN.

Other Considerations

There are other useful strategies to consider when designing a Conceptual Understanding Unit to best meet the learning needs of all secondary students. In the following section, we present a knowledge package idea that can be used along with the "unwrapping" process to pinpoint the particular concepts students need to learn in depth for a particular topic. To conclude this chapter, we provide a powerful process for vocabulary development, applicable not only to mathematics but also to all other content areas.

The Knowledge Package Process

The knowledge package process was listed earlier as the fourth step of the conceptual unit design sequence. It provides teachers with another effective method for determining the essential mathematical focus of a conceptual unit. Because the knowledge package process is worthy of consideration in and of itself, we include a separate description of it here.

In her book, *Knowing and Teaching Elementary Mathematics*, Liping Ma describes a *knowledge package* as a "group of topics that teachers tend to see around the topic they are teaching" (1999, p. 118). She states, "You should see a knowledge package when you are teaching a piece of knowledge. You have to know that the knowledge you are teaching is supported by [particular] ideas or procedures" (p. 18). For example, the operation of subtraction with regrouping (which Liping Ma refers to as "decomposition of numbers") is *the application of several ideas* rather than a single idea. "It is a package, rather than a sequence of knowledge" (p. 17).

We present the following knowledge package activity in our *Five Easy Steps to a Balanced Math Program* workshops to assist educators in identifying the essential mathematical understanding to be developed during a unit of study. This activity, usually completed by a grade-level, course, or department team of teachers planning together, helps teachers determine the understandings students must have to be successful with a particular math concept.

Make a *cluster* of the concepts, skills, and procedures that are related to a selected math topic.

> *You have to know that the knowledge you are teaching is supported by [particular] ideas or procedures.*
>
> —Liping Ma

Step 3: Conceptual Understanding

Decide which parts of the cluster are *procedural* and which are *conceptual*.

Discuss which parts of the cluster represent the *essential mathematical understandings* necessary for student success.

Use these essential mathematical understandings to help develop *Big Ideas* and *Essential Questions* for the conceptual unit.

For example, consider the topic of adding unlike fractions. Working together, teachers create a cluster that shows all the concepts, skills, ideas, and vocabulary that are connected to adding unlike fractions. Figure 3.2 is an example of this kind of knowledge package cluster.

In the second part of the activity, the teachers discuss the items in the cluster and decide which ones are most important for students to understand about the topic of adding unlike fractions. They ask: "What is the key concept? What do students need to understand to be successful with the process of adding fractions with unlike denominators?" Through this discussion, it will become evident that students need to understand the concept of part-whole relationships and why a common denominator is necessary when adding unlike fractions (when adding fractions, you can only combine the same-size pieces).

Many of the other parts of the cluster are taught procedurally. Usually teachers admit that addition of unlike fractions is typically taught as a mechanical procedure, whereby students are told to follow a precise set of sequenced steps. Typically students memorize those steps and follow them without really understanding what they are doing, or why. After further discussion, the teachers usually realize that for students to really understand the addition of unlike fractions, it is absolutely essential that they have a solid

Example of Knowledge Package Cluster	Figure 3.2

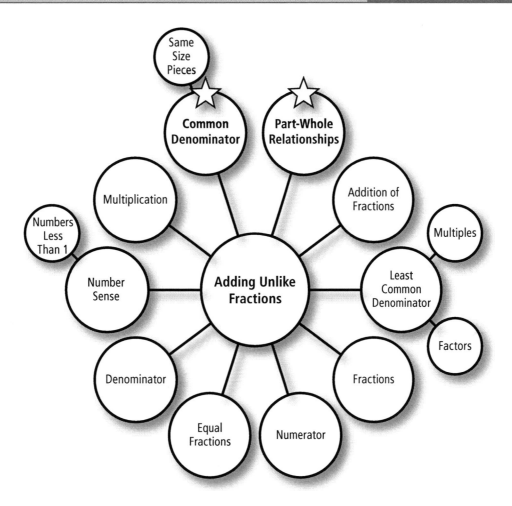

understanding of the concept of fractional numbers and what happens to those numbers when they are combined.

The main benefit of the knowledge package discussion activity is that it allows teachers to identify the *essential mathematical understandings* (Big Ideas) that they will then emphasize conceptually during a unit of study focused on the chosen topic. We urge secondary-grade teachers to try to create a knowledge package for a selected topic before planning the instructional lessons and activities for teaching that topic.

Differentiation and Vocabulary Development

The results of student assessment in mathematics are directly affected by student knowledge of mathematical vocabulary. In his book, *Building Background Knowledge for Academic Achievement*, Robert Marzano describes a six-step process for providing students with direct instruction in vocabulary.

The process involves the teacher describing vocabulary terms; students constructing their own descriptions of terms; students constructing nonlinguistic representations; the teacher providing opportunities for students to review and add to their knowledge of the terms; students interacting about the terms; and students playing games involving vocabulary terms (Marzano, 2004, p. 103).

Jan Christinson developed the following activity that applies Marzano's six-step process to increase student understanding of vocabulary—in this case, mathematical vocabulary. Students record their work in an "academic notebook," a journal in which they write initial definitions for vocabulary words and then continue to refine those definitions over time.

For example, let us use "circle" as the subject for this activity. The vocabulary words for this subject are *circle, diameter, radius, circumference, pi,* and *chord.* The procedure is as follows:

Step 1 Students individually cluster what they know about a circle. After clustering, each student shares his or her cluster with a partner and adds to his or her own cluster during the sharing.

Differentiation and Vocabulary Development

Step 2 The teacher presents to the class a teacher-made definition of each math word, and then repeats that definition. Students paraphrase the teacher's definition in writing and draw a graphic representation to match. After writing their paraphrased definitions, students discuss them with partners and revise if necessary. They then repeat the process for each of the words presented.

Step 3 Working in small groups of three or four, students create similes or metaphors for the vocabulary words and then share those with the class. Here are two examples:

  - A radius is like a spoke on a wheel.
  - Circumference is a snake biting its tail.

Step 4 After they complete the metaphor-and-simile activity, students revise their paraphrased definitions in their academic notebooks.

Step 5 While in the same groups, students play a pantomime game. One member of the group is chosen to act out one of the circle words. The other members of the group try to guess the word from the pantomimed visual clues.

Step 6 Without referring to their notes, students create a cluster to show all that they now know about a circle. After doing this, they self-reflect by referring to the notes they took during the earlier steps.

We encourage readers to experiment with this powerful activity to develop student knowledge of mathematical vocabulary.

Step 3: Conceptual Understanding

Locate the conceptual unit planning template in the "Reproducibles" section of this book. Working with your grade-level, course, or department colleagues, begin designing a math unit based on this conceptual unit model. First, determine your topic; then find the grade-specific standards or indicators that match. "Unwrap" the standards or indicators to find the concepts and skills. Apply the knowledge package process described earlier in this chapter. Decide on your Big Ideas and write your Essential Questions. Then, design an end-of-unit post-assessment directly aligned with your "unwrapped" concepts and skills and with your Big Ideas. Write the scoring guide that you will use to evaluate student performance on the post-assessment. After that, follow the remaining sequence of steps provided in this chapter, including the math vocabulary development suggestions.

Refer to the sample grade 6, grades 7 and 8, and high school conceptual units in Chapters 6, 7, and 8, respectively. Refer also to Chapter 9 for answers to frequently asked questions about step 3, Conceptual Understanding.

Step 4: Mastery of Math Facts

CHAPTER 4

Essential Questions

How do students learn their math facts? How should *they learn them?*

Do you have an accountability system in place so that students not only learn but also retain their math facts?

Has a timeline been established to determine when students will learn all their math facts?

Rationale

Just as learning to count is a prerequisite skill that very young children need before they can begin exploring and manipulating number concepts, mastery of basic number facts is necessary as students move through the first formal years of schooling. By the time students leave elementary school, they should have these facts firmly committed to memory—yet the majority of middle school teachers report that this is not the case.

The fourth step in our balanced math program suggests ways in which teachers can help their students master basic math facts *before* they enter middle school, and provides strategies that secondary-grade teachers can use to help students who are still struggling with those facts. Even though this fourth step of the *Five Easy Steps* program pertains mainly to elementary grades, we have chosen to include the information in this secondary edition, in the hope that the suggestions and strategies offered will be useful to middle school and high school math teachers whose students still do not know their basic math facts.

Students who do not learn their math facts have great difficulty solving problems accurately and in an appropriate amount of time.

Not only does this cause them frustration, but it also weakens their perception of themselves as mathematically powerful students, undermining the self-concept that we as educators are striving so diligently to promote and achieve through our unit planning, our engaging lessons and activities, and our methods of assessment.

Marilyn Burns has this to say with regard to students learning their basic number facts: "Memorization plays an important role in computation. Calculating mentally or with paper and pencil requires having basic number facts committed to memory. However, memorization should follow, not lead, instruction that builds children's understanding. The emphasis of learning in mathematics must always be on thinking, reasoning, and making sense" (1999, p. 408). How, then, do we help students master the necessary skill of being able to fluently and accurately recall their math facts?

Implementing Step 4

Emphasize Patterns

We have found that helping students discover patterns makes it easier and more interesting for them to learn and retain number facts. Therefore, we strive to create a classroom environment that emphasizes patterns, presents number facts in a way that makes sense, and reinforces fact acquisition through regular practice. Read what respected math researcher and author John Van De Walle has to say about teaching students math facts:

> *Fortunately, we know quite a bit about helping children develop fact mastery, and it has little to do with quantity of drill or drill*

techniques. Three components or steps to this end can be identified:

1. *Help children develop a strong understanding of the operations and of number relationships.*

2. *Develop efficient strategies for fact retrieval through practice.*

3. *Then provide drill in the use and selection of those strategies once they have been developed*

(Van De Walle, 2004, p. 157).

We recommend presenting lessons that demonstrate the various patterns in our number system. One method for doing this is to teach students the addition and subtraction "fact families":

$5 + 3 = 8$	$3 + 5 = 8$	$8 - 3 = 5$	$8 - 5 = 3$

and the multiplication and division "fact families":

$2 \times 3 = 6$	$3 \times 2 = 6$	$6 \div 3 = 2$	$6 \div 2 = 3$

Fact families help students recognize the unique relationships between the mathematical operations of addition and subtraction, multiplication and division. They help students understand that addition and subtraction, and multiplication and division, are inverse operations.

Another method to help children learn their multiplication facts is to teach them all the factors and factor combinations of a given number. By asking students to find all the ways to make 12 in multiplication (1×12, 2×6, 3×4, and so on), the teacher is also creating the perfect opportunity to introduce the concept of prime and composite numbers.

Fact families help students recognize the unique relationships between the mathematical operations of addition and subtraction, multiplication and division.

Discovering the patterns within products of multiplication facts is also helpful for children who are striving to learn their math facts. When students see that the products of all the fives, for example, can be found by skip-counting specific intervals of that number again and again, the stage is set for introducing students to the concept of multiples.

Once students feel comfortable with these patterns and can recall answers accurately, drill and practice using these strategies will help students become increasingly efficient in recalling basic facts. "Adopt this simple rule and stick with it: Do not subject any student to fact drills unless the student has developed an efficient strategy for the facts included in the drill" (Van De Walle, 2004, p. 174).

Determine Grade-Appropriate Facts

To determine *when* students should master their addition and subtraction facts in primary grades, and multiplication and division facts in upper elementary grades, start by referencing district and state mathematics standards and discussing grade-level expectations with colleagues. It is essential to agree upon this at the individual school site. When teachers decide together which facts should be learned in first grade, second grade, and so on, and then communicate these expectations to parents, the cumulative result at the end of elementary school is a body of students who know their facts!

Kindergarten students need lots of beginning practice with number combinations that make 5 and later 10. Typically, first-grade students work with addition facts up through 10, but the state standards may expect students to learn their facts up to and including 20. Teachers usually agree that a developmentally appropriate expectation for second-graders is that they learn addition *and* subtraction facts up to 20. Third-graders continue practicing addition and subtraction facts and begin learning easier multiplication facts (twos, threes, fours, fives, nines, and tens). They discover the relationship between addition and multiplication (repeated addition, such as $3 + 3 + 3$ representing three groups of three or $3 \times 3 = 9$). Fourth-graders maintain their fluency with addition and subtraction facts while also working to master the remaining multiplication facts and the corresponding division facts.

We believe that fifth grade is the year when students need to demonstrate that they have mastered the number facts in all four basic operations. Fifth-graders are on the verge of entering middle school mathematics classes, where such prior learning is expected. Therefore, we hold them more rigorously accountable than we do younger children.

The "Reproducibles" section at the end of this book includes a summary of the patterns we recommend emphasizing in each grade, K–5, along with suggestions for helping students learn their facts both at school and at home. Many of these suggestions will be useful to middle school teachers for use with students who still do not know their math facts.

Inform Parents at Beginning of Year

Parents can play a major role in helping their children practice and learn basic math facts. Parents understand the importance of learning math facts because they once had to learn them, too! Students know that they need to learn their math facts—teachers tell them so every year—yet not all students motivate themselves

> *We believe that fifth grade is the year when students need to demonstrate that they have mastered the number facts in all four basic operations.*

We also believe in keeping parents informed of their children's progress as the year continues by sending home the results of each math-facts assessment.

to do so. Parental support and assistance are therefore essential, and it is up to the teacher to communicate the need for that support and then establish a program of accountability to ensure that each student receives it. Traditional events at the beginning of the school year, such as Back-to-School Night and distribution of the teacher's welcome letter, provide excellent opportunities to inform parents of the specific math facts their children will need to learn that year.

Establish Timeline to Assess Progress

At the beginning of a school year, we allow two or three months of practice before holding students accountable by means of a math-facts assessment. After that, we establish a regular assessment schedule as described later in this chapter.

It is important to let parents know how often students will be assessed for fact recall. Our experience has been that with a regular system of accountability (a weekly or biweekly quiz, for example), there is a much greater likelihood that students and parents will make the mastery of facts a priority.

We also believe in keeping parents informed of their children's progress as the year continues by sending home the results of each math-facts assessment. We require students who do not demonstrate mastery on those periodic assessments to do extra practice nightly until mastery is achieved and verified through subsequent reassessment.

Assess What Students Presently Know

When beginning your program to promote mastery of math facts, first assess what students currently know, by using a written or oral quiz. Thereafter, systematically build into the math program regular opportunities for children to practice facts, in as nonthreatening a climate as possible. As described later, the Math Review and Mental Math portions of the daily math period provide excellent practice opportunities for students to do this.

In both primary and upper elementary grades, teachers generally use their own self-made assessments, commercially produced assessments, or both. Whatever the format used, and regardless of whether that format is used in only one classroom or across several grade levels within a school, our recommendation is to choose a format that works and use it consistently.

Provide Daily Practice Materials

The key to unlocking student success with math facts, *before* formal testing, is regular, systematic practice, both in school and at home. Here are several suggestions for helping upper elementary (and middle school) students master their number facts with home and in-school practice:

Orally practice all the twos, threes, fours, etc., with a family member, classmate, or teacher aide. Focus first on the groupings of like facts or sequential groupings; then at random; and finally with all the facts mixed together.

Use flash cards to practice all the twos, threes, fours, etc., with a family member, classmate, or teacher aide. Focus first on the groupings of like facts or sequential groupings, then at random, and then all together.

Notice product patterns for multiplication:

- Look at product patterns for five (0, 5, 10, 15, 20, 25, 30, 35, 40, 45) in which the ones digit alternates between zero and five.

The key to unlocking student success with math facts, before formal testing, is regular, systematic practice, both in school and at home.

- Look at product patterns for three (3, 6, 9, where 3 + 6 = 9) and the remaining products (12, 15, 18, 21, 24, 27) in which the sum of the two digits equals three, six, or nine.

- Look at product patterns of nine (9, 18, 27, 36, 45, 54, 63, 72, 81, 90) in which the sum of the two digits equals nine; the tens digits are sequenced in order from one to nine; and the ones digits are sequenced in reverse, from nine to zero).

Count aloud the multiples of a given number.

Learn the fact families in addition, subtraction, multiplication, and division.

Write math facts each day in school and at home.

Play math-facts games on the Internet and utilize computer software math-facts programs.

Use practice worksheets.

Read literature books that involve adding, subtracting, multiplying, and dividing in the story line.

Math Review and Mental Math

Math Review and Mental Math also provide excellent opportunities for students to practice and learn their math facts, while they solve procedural math problems or mentally calculate a sequence of numbers and operations. Number sense and math facts are reinforced and developed when teachers emphasize "reasonable answer" and the different ways to solve a problem during the processing of Math Review and Mental Math. Students learn to use the facts they know to find the facts they are not sure of. Developing a strong understanding of the number system and its patterns will help students develop confidence in the other areas of mathematics.

A Simple Management System

Regular administration of math-facts assessments can be a demanding task, especially if the teacher has to score all the papers, keep track of which students need to be reassessed, and then schedule those assessments (including makeups for absent students). We have used the following system with excellent results.

We set up an expanding file system, using Pendaflex folders or something similar, and label the different folders according to the specific facts for addition, subtraction, multiplication, and division. We keep the files stocked with copies of the initial assessment, practice papers for homework, and subsequent assessments. Students can be taught how to go to the files and select the particular assessment they need.

Helping Students Handle Time Pressure

Most students like the challenge of writing the sum or difference under an addition or subtraction fact problem and the product or quotient under a multiplication or division problem. Ask students to perform within a limited time, under time constraints, and that enjoyment remains high for those who love challenges—but it plummets drastically for those who do not. All the rationale

Step 4: Mastery of Math Facts

Timed testing does not teach students math facts. Students learn math facts from good instruction.

in the world about why these assessments should be timed prove ineffective when students are trying their best to perform, but just cannot get those answers on the paper fast enough.

How fast should students be expected to perform accurately on a math-facts assessment? This is an issue to be decided by individual teachers, grade levels, or the entire school. Caring as teachers do about promoting positive self-esteem in the mathematics classroom, it seems counterproductive to apply a time constraint to the administration of an assessment, knowing the effect it will have on certain students. Consider the words of Marilyn Burns on the subject of timed tests:

> Teachers who use timed tests believe that the tests help children learn basic facts. This perspective makes no instructional sense. Children who perform well under time pressure display their skills. Children who have difficulty with skills, or who work more slowly, run the risk of reinforcing wrong practices under pressure. Also, they can become fearful about, and negative toward, their mathematics learning (Burns, 1999, p. 408).

Timed tests are a traditional method of math assessment, but alternate methods should be made available to students who are greatly frustrated by a time constraint. A timed test is an *assessment*; it is not instruction. Timed testing does not teach students math facts. Students learn math facts from good instruction. Nevertheless, a long-standing practice in American education has been to assess student recall of math facts within predetermined time limits. For teachers who decide that they must continue requiring students to complete a certain number of problems within a specified time limit, we offer the following suggestions for doing so.

When It Is Time to Start Assessing

The first week you plan to assess, send home a letter on Monday to inform parents that your math-facts accountability program is beginning. Give each student a copy of the number facts you have selected to quiz. Tell the class that they will use this paper to practice during the coming week. Announce that on Friday you will give them a clean copy of the same paper, or a different sequence of the same problems that they have studied, to be completed without help within so many minutes. Let them know how much time they will have, and allow them to practice once or twice together so that they can experience working within a time limit before taking the actual quiz.

Urge students to practice at home with their parents every night and to use word and number associations or other creative ways to remember the facts that are difficult for them. Remind them of the patterns they have learned. Remind them also that they have practiced these facts in fun ways at school and at home, and that they already know many of these facts. Encourage them to take a practice quiz at home within the predetermined time limit, so that they simulate the assessment conditions. Announce your criteria for proficient performance. Throughout the week, and even before the assessment on Friday, orally review the facts you will be assessing.

Assessment Day

Distribute a copy of the assessment to each student. Direct students to write their names on their papers, turn their papers over, and wait for the "go" signal. Students often enjoy the synchronized swishing sound when the entire class turns over papers at once and begins. Mark time in minutes, writing the elapsed time on the

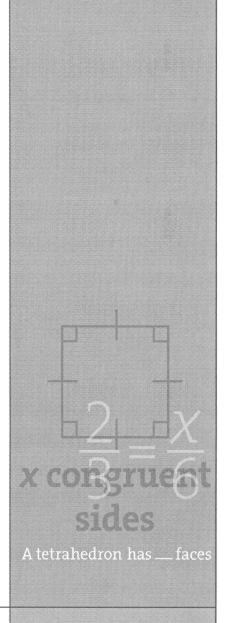

$$\frac{2}{3} = \frac{x}{6}$$

x congruent sides

A tetrahedron has __ faces

board for anyone who wants to see. We suggest *not* calling out the time remaining, as this seems to put extra stress on many students.

When 30 seconds remain in the allotted time, direct students to stop, hold their pencils in the air, look down at their papers, and determine how many more facts they need to do. Then, announce that 30 seconds remain and encourage students to write as many more answers in the time left as they can. This seems to help focus students and prepare them for the impending "time's up" announcement.

Scoring, Collecting, and Recording Results

At the conclusion of the allotted quiz time, direct students to exchange papers. Instruct them to mark only the incorrect answers as you both say the answers aloud and write them on an overhead transparency of the actual quiz, one row of answers at a time. By looking at the answers projected on the board or screen, students can self-correct the papers they are scoring if they lose track of the answers the teacher is giving verbally.

Collect only the papers that achieve or exceed the passing score you predetermined and announced in advance to students. Instruct the rest of the students to keep their papers and continue practicing for the next quiz. Record the scores of only those students who passed this particular quiz.

Once you begin assessing students on their math facts, continue this procedure weekly or biweekly so that students regard it as an ongoing, regular part of their balanced math program. These assessments will allow students and parents to gauge progress toward the end goal of mastering *all* the grade-level facts they are responsible for learning that year.

Periodically reassess students who have already demonstrated mastery to make sure they still know their facts. Holding students accountable for fact mastery throughout the school year promotes long-term retention.

Holding students accountable for fact mastery throughout the school year promotes long-term retention.

Extra Practice Required

As indicated earlier, we always notify parents of students who do not show an acceptable level of proficiency on a particular math-facts assessment; we also provide them with suggested strategies to help their children become successful. Students are reassessed on these same math facts until they demonstrate proficiency.

Reassessing

We suggest three approaches to reassessing. Because these suggestions would not be necessary or even appropriate for entire classes of secondary students, middle school math teachers might want to consider using any of these approaches for small groups of struggling students.

The first approach is to reassess individual students on the same facts the following week, while those who did pass take the next assessment in the sequence. This focuses each student's attention on mastering one set of facts before moving on to the next.

The second approach is to allow individual students to do a reassessment during the coming week and take the next assessment in the sequence along with the rest of the class on the following Friday. This works well for students who want to keep pace with their classmates, but it may put too much pressure on those who are having difficulty remembering their facts.

The third way is to take the entire group of students through the sequence of facts they need to learn and then go back and reassess students on the particular facts they have yet to master. This approach often works best, because it provides ongoing review of all the facts and prevents low-performing students from feeling that they are behind the rest of the group.

Differentiation: Strategies for Struggling Students

Secondary students who are struggling to learn their math facts will benefit from a different approach. More drill is not the answer! Here are a few suggestions that should prove effective:

Help these students find out which facts they know and which facts they do not. Many students who are struggling or who have become overly frustrated think that they do not know any math facts. This is certainly not true, and teachers need to help these students realize this.

Reemphasize patterns within the number system and help students see that math facts are interconnected.

Find out if the student has a strategy of his or her own that he or she uses to find the answer to an unknown fact. Share among students any of these helpful strategies based on patterns that other students are using.

Involve students in daily Mental Math activities to help them develop their number sense.

Summing Up

Provide students with frequent opportunities to experience success. One way to do this is to focus on a few related math facts at a time. When frustrated students experience even a little success, it can begin to change their entire attitude toward math!

Offer alternate methods of assessing math-facts proficiency (use of flash cards, oral responses, individual assessment, and so on).

Allow use of the calculator during problem-solving activities (not to compute simple math-fact answers, but as a tool to assist students while solving multistep problems).

Summing Up

It *is* possible to help all students achieve mastery of their basic math facts. Teachers who have been the most successful in producing students who can recall math facts follow this proven three-part formula:

1. Teach math facts in the context of patterns, using the strategies provided earlier in this chapter.
2. Provide ongoing practice, both in and out of the classroom.
3. Establish a regular timeline for assessing math facts; then inform parents and enlist their support.

Step 4: Mastery of Math Facts

Plan how you will incorporate the recommendations described in this chapter into your balanced math program.

1. *Determine the grade-appropriate facts you want your students to master.*

2. *Consider how you will teach math facts through patterns.*

3. *Establish a timeline for regular assessment of student progress and then draft your letter to parents.*

4. *Select your math-facts assessment program and gather necessary instructional and practice materials.*

5. *Reflect on the other suggestions included in this chapter to help you implement this component of your balanced math program.*

6. *Refer again to the "Reproducibles" section at the end of the book for a summary of the patterns we recommend to assist students in learning their math facts in each grade, K–5. Refer also to Chapter 9 for answers to frequently asked questions about step 4, Mastery of Math Facts.*

Step 5: Common Formative Assessment

CHAPTER 5

Essential Questions

How are you assessing the effectiveness of math instruction within your grade level, department, school, or district throughout the school year?

How frequently are you collecting student data from math assessments, and how are you using this data to improve student achievement?

Overview

Common formative assessments are assessments collaboratively designed by a grade-level, course, or department team of teachers and administered to all of the students in that grade level, course, or department several times throughout the school year. Teachers use the results of common formative assessment to evaluate student understanding of the essential standards they are currently teaching. Because these assessments are formative by design and intent, they provide participating teachers with the timely feedback needed to differentiate instruction and thus better meet the diverse learning needs of their students. In this way, assessment truly informs instruction.

Grade-level, course, or department teachers often collaboratively score their common formative assessments, analyze the results together, and discuss ways to achieve improvements in student learning on the next common formative assessment. These instruments are typically designed to be used as both a pre- and a post-assessment (to ensure same-assessment to same-assessment comparison). Thus, participating teachers administer their common formative pre- and post-assessments to measure student growth in understanding from the beginning of an instructional unit (of approximately two to four weeks' duration) until its end. If these in-school, common *formative* assessments are also aligned to the large-scale district and state *summative* assessments, the formative assessment results will reveal what students still need to learn to be successful on those external assessments. These internal assessments thus provide valuable diagnostic information in time for teachers to make needed instructional changes.

Rationale

Most educators agree that the usefulness of data from the annual state assessments is limited, because state data offer only a limited view of how a particular child performed on a given day rather than providing a window into student understanding as viewed over time.

The external state assessment is an assessment *of* students' learning that is summative, whereas the internal classroom assessment is an assessment *for* students' learning that is formative (Stiggins, Arter, Chappuis, & Chappuis, 2004). However, both types of assessment are necessary. "Assessment must be seen as an *instructional tool* for use while learning is occurring and as an *accountability tool* to determine if learning has occurred" (NEA, 2003). The National Education Association report also explained why formative assessments *for* learning are so vital to students:

> In the context of classroom assessment, however, one key purpose can be to use assessment results to inform students about themselves. That is, classroom assessments can inform students about the continuous improvements in their achievement and

permit them to feel in control of that growth. Thus, classroom assessments become assessments for learning. Teachers involve their students in the classroom assessment process for the express purpose of increasing their achievement (NEA, 2003).

Power Standards

The daunting number of academic content standards that students are expected to learn each year presents a formidable challenge to teachers whose primary responsibility it is to impart all those standards to their students. Teachers must also determine the progress students are making toward proficiency with these many standards, and they need to be able to make sound decisions based on the data they collect. With so many learning objectives to teach and assess, how can teachers do this effectively?

One important way they can narrow their instruction and assessment focus is to identify the Power Standards: a *prioritized* subset of the entire list of standards that represents the essential concepts and skills students must understand and be able to demonstrate competency in by the end of each school year, prekindergarten through grade 12 (Ainsworth, 2003a).

Educational researcher Robert Marzano provided the following data to estimate the amount of time it would take to effectively teach all the standards students are expected to learn by the end of high school:

- 5.6 instructional hours per day × 180 days in a typical academic year = 1,008 hours per year × 13 years = <u>13,104</u> total hours of K−12 instruction.

- Mid-continent Research for Education and Learning (McREL) identified 200 standards and 3,093 benchmarks in national- and state-level documents across 14 different subject areas.

- Classroom teachers estimated a need for 15,465 hours to adequately teach them all (Marzano, 2003, pp. 24–25).

Further, Marzano revealed a powerful reality check regarding how many of those instructional hours each school day are actually devoted to instruction of students:

- Varies widely from a low of 21 percent to a high of 69 percent

- Taking the highest estimate of 69 percent, only 9,042 hours are actually available for instruction out of the original 13,104 hours total.

- 200 standards and 3,093 benchmarks requiring 15,465 instructional hours cannot be thoroughly taught in only 9,042 hours of instructional time (Marzano, 2003, pp. 24–25).

Marzano concluded his statistics with a memorable bit of logic: "To cover all this content, you would have to change schooling from K-12 to K-22." He recommends a fractional guideline for reducing the number of standards—"By my reckoning, we would have to cut content by about two-thirds"—and ends with a dramatic assertion: "The sheer number of standards is the biggest impediment to implementing standards" (Marzano, 2001, p. 15).

Power Standards are *not* the only standards educators teach in any given content area. The other standards must also be taught, but a clear distinction is made as to which standards require the greatest amount of instructional time and emphasis. Vertically aligned from one grade to the next, these prioritized standards represent what

Vertical Alignment

all students must know and be able to do in order to be successful —in school each year, in life, and on all high-stakes assessments. Power Standards provide the laser-like focus teachers need to develop instructional units and the corresponding assessments to determine student proficiency on those essential standards.

Common formative assessments, when collaboratively designed, administered, scored, and analyzed, are directly aligned to the Power Standards *only.* Because these assessments are formative, grade-level, course, or department teams of teachers can use the results to differentiate and improve instruction of those standards critical for all-round student success.

Vertical Alignment

An invaluable activity to enhance the conceptual unit building process described in step 3 and the development of common formative assessments described later in this chapter is to involve grade-level teams of teachers first in selecting and then in vertically aligning their math Power Standards. Working in grade-level teams (elementary) and course or department teams (secondary), each grade level decides the essential mathematical skills and concepts students need for success in each grade level and course. They then vertically align those selected Power Standards from one grade level to the next, both *within* each span of grades (preK–2, 3–5, 6–8, and 9–12) and then *between* each grade span (2–3, 5–6, 8–9), until there is a "vertical flow" of all the standards considered essential for students to know and be able to do by the end of high school.

Step 5: Common Formative Assessment

To accomplish this, teachers rely first upon their professional judgment and classroom experience, and use the selection criteria of endurance, leverage, and readiness for the next level of learning to make their Power Standards selections. The easiest way to do this is to consider what students need to know and be able to do to be mathematically successful (1) in school each year; (2) in life; and (3) on the annual state assessment. Beginning in one particular strand of mathematics (e.g., geometry, algebra, data, measurement, number, etc.), teachers reach initial consensus among themselves as to which standards for each individual grade are the "power" ones. Next, they cross-reference district or state standards and their annual state assessment data to check that their selections match the concepts and skills most heavily emphasized on the state test; they then modify the selections as needed. After that, they chart their selections by grade level and post them on the wall in consecutive sequence from prekindergarten through high school grades.

The preK–12 group then examines the selections from one grade to the next, looking across the charts to trace the development of key concepts and skills across the span of grade levels and courses. During their discussions, the participating teachers look for gaps from one level to the next and make changes on the charts to address specific gaps as needed.

This *gap analysis* process is extremely valuable. For example, a preK–12 team in a midwestern state was examining vertically aligned Power Standards selections in the number-sense strand. The fifth-grade team of teachers noticed an apparent break in the conceptual development of fractions, which occurred in both second and third grades. The grade 5 teachers knew that systematic development of students' understanding of fractions was a critical concept for student success at their grade level. Without the development of fractional understanding *in each and every grade* below grade 5, students would not come to grade 5 with the necessary prerequisite understanding of fractions. After this discovery was brought to everyone's attention, the teachers in grades 2 and 3 willingly revised their number-strand selections so that the flow of fractional development continued throughout all elementary years. The middle school teachers present were very encouraged by this, knowing how critical a solid understanding of fractional concepts is to student success in middle school mathematics.

The identification of preK–12 math Power Standards helps all teachers in every grade level and course know exactly which standards they must emphasize in order to develop in-depth student understanding. These Power Standards become the central focus for conceptual unit building (described in Chapter 3) and for the development of common formative assessments aligned to those conceptual units.

Readers interested in learning more about the process for identifying Power Standards, not only in math but in all content areas, will find this information fully described with accompanying district examples in *Power Standards: Identifying the Standards That Matter the Most* (Ainsworth, 2003a), and in the publications of educational author and researcher, Douglas B. Reeves.

The identification of preK–12 math Power Standards helps all teachers in every grade level and course know exactly which standards they must emphasize in order to develop in-depth student understanding.

Beginning with the End in Mind

Ideally, grade-level or department math teachers will collaboratively design common formative assessments to administer to all their students several times a year. Teachers can use the pre-assessment results to improve instructional planning within their own individual classrooms. Knowing—in advance—what will be required of their students on the common formative math *post*-assessment, they can plan the instruction, lessons, and informal classroom assessments needed to prepare students for success on that common formative post-assessment. This "backwards planning" (Wiggins & McTighe, 1998) approach will greatly assist teachers in keeping their instruction closely aligned to their common assessments.

As teachers informally assess their students throughout the conceptual unit, they will gain diagnostic information as to what their students still need to know and be able to do. This information will help them monitor and adjust instruction *before* students take the end-of-unit classroom assessment and the common formative post-assessment. If teachers use the assessment results at each stage of the process to adjust instruction as needed, these aligned classroom and grade-level assessments become extremely valuable for informing and differentiating instruction.

Designing the Common Formative Assessment

Common formative assessments can be very similar in design to the end-of-unit classroom assessments. A grade-level or department team of teachers that has already collaboratively designed a conceptual unit assessment for a key mathematical topic can design a similar version of that same assessment as a common formative assessment. The teachers emphasize the same key concepts and skills, but change the problems. They all administer the common assessment to their students as soon as instruction and the learning activities for the unit are completed.

More often, however, grade-level teams design a different common formative assessment that includes a blend of items, including both selected-response questions (multiple choice, short answer, matching) and constructed-response questions (Problem-Solving Task). The common assessment may also include problems from more than one math standard or strand. Whereas the classroom end-of-unit assessment (as shown in the step 3 example in Chapter 3) is more performance-based (a Problem-Solving Task), the common formative assessment may also include computation problems matched to the Power Standards targeted during one or more conceptual units. Such common assessments require students to demonstrate both their procedural understanding *and* their conceptual understanding. In this way, the assessment provides teachers with a multiple-measure insight into students' understanding.

The Implementation Sequence

Here is a recommended sequence of steps to follow when a secondary grade-level, course, or department team of teachers decides to design and administer a common formative math assessment. Note that the common formative assessment is designed as both a pre- and a post-assessment, so that teachers can use the *pre*-assessment results to determine how best to meet student learning needs

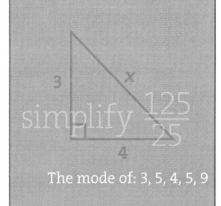

during the upcoming unit of instruction, and then use the *post-*assessment results at the end of the unit to measure the learning gains made by each student.

1. *Identify the math Power Standards* for each grade level and course, preK–12. (This is usually done as a district-wide process, but it can be done within an individual school. In this example, a middle school determines its math Power Standards for grades 6–8, whereas a high school determines its math Power Standards for the individual courses that students take in a prescribed sequence.)

2. *Within grade-level, course, or department teams, determine an important math topic to teach conceptually in the classroom.* Locate that topic in the identified math Power Standards.

3. *"Unwrap" those Power Standards* (as described in Chapter 3) to pinpoint the concepts and skills students need to know and be able to do.

4. *Determine the Big Ideas and Essential Questions* from the "unwrapped" Power Standards.

5. *Collaboratively design common formative pre- and post-assessments* that are aligned to one another, to evaluate student understanding of the "unwrapped" Power Standards, concepts, skills, and Big Ideas for that important topic.

6. *Design a classroom end-of-unit assessment and scoring guide* matched to the common formative assessment.

7. *Plan the classroom conceptual unit of instruction,* making sure it is aligned with the end-of-unit assessment.

8. *Administer and score the common formative pre-assessment* and analyze the results in grade-level, course, or department Data Teams. (*Note: Data Teams* are collaborative teams of teachers who teach the same grade level or math course. They use a simple, five-step process to chart student data, analyze the data, set a team goal, select effective teaching strategies, and develop an action plan. For more information on the Data Team process, please contact the Center for Performance Assessment at 1-800-844-6599 or visit its Website at www.MakingStandardsWork.com).

9. *Teach the conceptual units of instruction* in each classroom. Assess informally throughout the unit and adjust instruction accordingly.

10. *Administer and score the common formative post-assessment* and analyze the results in grade-level, course, or department Data Teams.

The Big Picture—How All the Practices Connect

Here is an additional sequence of steps that shows how to align the school-based common formative assessments with district and state assessments. Following that is a diagram that represents the connections between each of the practices described in this chapter (Figure 5.1). This information is relevant for all elementary and secondary teachers, math grade-level and department chairs, and school leaders, because it represents the "big-picture" alignment of preK–12 math standards and assessments and shows the connections between particular components of *Five Easy Steps* and those practices.

Step 5: Common Formative Assessment

1. *Align common formative assessments* in each school with quarterly district benchmark assessments (elementary/secondary) and end-of-course assessments (secondary).

2. *Administer quarterly district benchmark assessments;* analyze those results (whether formative or summative) in Data Teams to inform current and future instruction and assessment.

3. *Align quarterly district benchmark and end-of-course assessments* with the annual state assessments. (*Note:* Educators do this by referencing (1) state assessment requirements, (2) current-year and prior-year school and district state test data, and (3) released state assessment items and formats from prior years. This enables the educators to better prepare students for what will be expected of them on the annual state assessments.)

Figure 5.1 shows how all these practices interconnect. Note the double-headed arrow on the elementary district benchmark assessments; this indicates that the assessments can be either formative or summative. The single-headed arrow pointing to the end-of-course secondary assessments indicates that these assessments are summative only.

Readers interested in more detailed information about the collaborative design, administration, scoring, and analysis of common formative assessments, as the centerpiece of an integrated instruction and assessment system, will find a complete description of each of these interrelated practices in *Common Formative Assessments: How to Connect Standards-based Instruction and Assessment* (Ainsworth & Viegut, 2006).

| Five Easy Steps Balanced Math Alignment Diagram | Figure 5.1 |

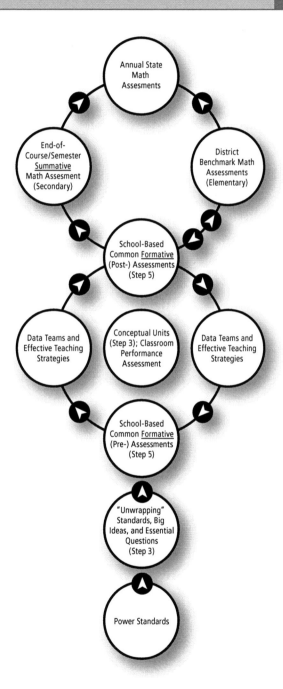

Adapted from *Common Formative Assessments: How to Connect Standards-Based Instruction and Assessment* (Ainsworth & Viegut, Corwin Press, 2006).

Implementation

Today's teachers and leaders have more to do than ever before. The resistance to implementing one more professional practice, however beneficial, often proves a difficult hurdle to overcome. The key here is relevance. If teachers see the direct connection of a new practice to improvement in student learning, they are usually willing to experiment with it in their own classrooms.

We recommend first "weeding the garden" of time-consuming activities that may prevent teachers from focusing on new practices that really will improve instruction and student learning. Once the ground has been cleared, then introduce the new practices; allow everyone time to try them out, and then gather together to discuss their effectiveness. If teachers see firsthand the value of those recommended new practices, discussions will naturally turn to effective implementation of them within the school's established instruction and assessment culture.

An excellent way to introduce each of the *Five Easy Steps* and related practices described in these pages is to start by taking small steps. Rather than attempting to simultaneously implement each of the five steps, while at the same time identifying Power Standards and forming Data Teams, choose one of these practices and focus on understanding and implementing that one first. When that practice is solidly in place, implement the next one; then continue through the remaining practices. In this way, teachers can effectively evaluate the worth of each of these interdependent practices. In less time than initially expected, all of these practices can put be in place and start working together to improve student achievement in math!

Benefits

Common formative assessments can greatly improve instruction and corresponding student achievement. Among their several important benefits are:

Regular and timely feedback regarding student attainment of the most essential math standards, so teachers can better meet the learning needs of all students

Multiple-measure assessments that allow students to demonstrate their understanding in a variety of formats

Ongoing collaboration opportunities for secondary math teachers who teach the same grade levels or courses

Consistent expectations within a grade level and within a grade span regarding standards, instruction, and assessment priorities

Established criteria for proficiency, to be met within each individual classroom, grade level, department, school, and district

Deliberate preparation for students to be successful through the intentional alignment of classroom and school assessments with external district and state assessments

Teachers well know that it always takes a lot of work to institute any new program or practice. The positive results to be gained by students indeed justify the time and effort required by the adults in the system to achieve those results. As you implement—over time—each of the *Five Easy Steps to a Balanced Math Program*, you will see for yourself a dramatic increase in student achievement. Even more importantly, you are likely to witness students' perceptions of their ability to "do math" shifting slowly but surely in the right direction. How rewarding it is for hard-working teachers to see students beginning to think of themselves as mathematically powerful!

In the next three chapters, we show the application of the *Five Easy Steps* in each of the secondary grades: grade 6, grades 7 and 8, and high school.

Reader's Assignment

Discuss these ideas with grade-level, course, and department colleagues. Talk with your administrator to request collaborative planning time to first identify the math Power Standards and then develop a common formative assessment matched to a particular math topic of importance. Progressing at a pace appropriate for you and your colleagues, follow the suggested sequence of steps described in this chapter for designing common formative assessments.

PART TWO

Inside the
Secondary Classroom

Inside the Grade 6 Classroom

CHAPTER

6

In this chapter, we show the application of the five steps of the balanced math program model in a grade 6 classroom. The examples provided illustrate Math Review, Mental Math, problem solving, and a Conceptual Understanding Unit. In addition, we have included information regarding the teaching of math facts, even though we recognize that mastery of math facts is an elementary school responsibility. We hope these grade-specific examples will benefit sixth-grade teachers in implementing these important balanced math program steps!

Step 1: Sixth-Grade Computational Skills (Math Review and Mental Math)

The Math Review Template

Math Review, as described in Chapter 1, occurs daily at the beginning of the math period. Sixth-graders complete the five problems independently using paper and pencil. However, teachers will certainly need to make whatever modifications are necessary to ensure that students can be successful working on their own.

Using the Math Review template, teachers either write the problems on the board for students to copy or prepare an individual worksheet for each student.

Inside the Grade 6 Classroom

To complete Math Review within the allotted time frame . . . we suggest fully processing only two or three different problems each day.

1. Place in order: -2, $4\frac{1}{2}$, 1, $.5$, $.25$

Number Sense

2. $3 \times \frac{3}{4} =$ _____

Fractions

3. $20 \div .5 =$ _____

Decimals

4. 75% of $40 =$ _____

Explain and solve

Percentage Unit

5. Find mean and median: 50, 65, 70, 75, 85, 15

Data

6.

Bonus

PROCESSING SEQUENCE. In this section are suggested strategies teachers can emphasize, during the processing of Math Review problems, to develop students' number sense and mathematical reasoning. Teachers can refer to these processing examples when developing their own strategies for processing Math Review problems. To complete Math Review within the allotted time frame, however, we suggest fully processing only two or three different problems each day. Provide just the answers for the others. There is not enough time to use every processing strategy for every problem every day, but do be sure to include *all* of these processing strategies over the course of each week. For the bonus problem, ask those students who solved it to orally state their answer along with a brief description of how they solved it.

Step 1: Sixth-Grade Computational Skills
(Math Review and Mental Math)

1. For the **Number Sense** problem:
   - The correct answer is $-2, .25, .5, 1, 4\frac{1}{2}$
   - Ask students what methods they could use to put the numbers in order from smallest to largest (e.g., convert decimals into fractions; convert fractions into decimals)
   - Ask students the special names for each number (negative integer, mixed number, whole number, decimal number)

2. For the **Fractions** problem:
   - The product is $2\frac{1}{4}$
   - Ask students what the algorithm means (3 groups of $\frac{3}{4}$)
   - Ask students for a reasonable answer (an answer less than 3)
   - Ask students how they might solve the problem mentally
   - Ask them to share different ways that they process $\frac{3}{4} + \frac{3}{4} + \frac{3}{4}$ mentally
   - Demonstrate a typical procedural method for multiplying a whole number and a fraction

3. For the **Decimals** problem:
   - The quotient is 40
   - Ask students what the problem means (how many groups of .5 are in 20)
   - Ask students how they might compute the problem mentally
   - Ask students for a reasonable answer or estimate (would have to be more than 20, because you are dividing by a number that is less than one)

- Ask students to "think multiplication" to find an answer or get close to an answer (what multiplied by $\frac{1}{2}$ would give an answer of 20?)

- Demonstrate the procedural method for moving the decimal out of the divisor

- Ask students why the decimal is moved (easier to divide by whole number)

4. For the **Percentage Unit** problem:

- The answer is 30

- Ask students what 75% means (75 out of 100)

- Ask students what fraction 75% represents ($\frac{75}{100}$ or $\frac{3}{4}$)

- Ask students for a reasonable answer (a number between 20 and 40)

- Ask students to solve $\frac{3}{4}$ of 40 mentally (30)

- Demonstrate the procedural method for multiplying a percentage of a whole number

5. For the **Data** problem:

- The answers are: mean is 60; median is 67.5

- Ask students for definitions of *mean* (find the sum of the data and divide by the number of items) and *median* (center of the data listed in numerical order)

- Ask students why mean or median might be the same or different. (Mean is affected the most by extreme data, such as the 15 in the given problem. Median is not affected by extreme data.)

Step 1: Sixth-Grade Computational Skills
(Math Review and Mental Math)

The Math Review Quiz

The Math Review Quiz becomes a biweekly assessment of students' computational understanding. Its purpose is to assess students on a regular basis to determine their proficiency with the types of problems they are practicing daily during Math Review. Note that there are *two* problems for each type of daily problem the students have been practicing throughout the week.

1. Place in order (smallest to largest): $0, 1, -3, .75, 3\frac{1}{2}$

2. Place in order (smallest to largest): $-2, 4\frac{3}{4}, -4, .80, 14$

3. $4 \times \frac{1}{4} = $ _____

4. $12 \times \frac{3}{4} = $ _____

5. $40 \div .8 = $ _____

6. $60 \div .5 = $ _____

7. 60% of 60 = _____ Solve and explain

8. 75% of 120 = _____ Solve and explain

9. Find mean and median: 60, 65, 65, 85, 75, 70

10. Find mean and median: 80, 70, 65, 85, 80, 60, 50

Mental Math

Mental Math should be matched to the content of Math Review. Regular practice will help develop students' number sense. Here are three examples of Mental Math problems that are appropriate for grade 6, with incremental answers provided. The word "equals" signals students to say or write the answer (provided in the last parenthetical of the problem in each of the following examples). Note also the Mental Math themes for each particular type of problem. Sixth-grade teachers may use these examples as guidelines for developing their own Mental Math problems.

Mental Math should be matched to the content of Math Review. Regular practice will help develop students' number sense.

EXAMPLES

"Start with 7×8 (56); add 4 (60); divide by 6 (10); take the answer to the second power (100); add 40 (140); subtract 80 (60); equals _____ ."

(Themes: mixed operations, basic facts)

"Start with $\frac{1}{4}$ of 12 (3); $\frac{1}{3}$ of the answer (1); $\frac{1}{2}$ of answer ($\frac{1}{2}$); square that number ($\frac{1}{4}$); equals _____ ."

(Theme: fractional parts of a whole)

"Start with the number of degrees in a circle (360); add the number of degrees in a right angle (450); divide by the number of sides on a pentagon (90); divide by the number of sides on a triangle (30); equals _____ ."

(Theme: geometry)

Step 2: Sixth-Grade Problem Solving

Sample Grade 6 Problem-Solving Task

The following is a sample Problem-Solving Task from the Website of the Math Forum @ Drexel (http://mathforum.org/pow/), an excellent problem-solving resource for teachers. The Forum's Problem of the Week service provides challenging, nonroutine word problems for students to solve online in a mentored environment. This particular problem is matched to the strand or standard of *geometry*. It was selected to align with the Conceptual Understanding Unit shown in step 3 (see next section). A student solution to the task appears after the problem. Readers may want to solve the problem themselves before taking a look at the solution. These problems can be quite challenging!

MATH FORUM PROBLEM-SOLVING TASK

553: Cubic Changes

Let's do a little more work with measurements today.

We'll begin with a cube that measures two centimeters on each edge. This cube will have a surface area of 24 square centimeters, and it will have a volume of 8 cubic centimeters.

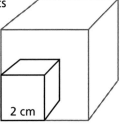

2 cm

What will happen to the area and volume if the edge of the cube is doubled?

Bonus: Let's see if we can generalize. What will happen to the area and volume of any cube if the length of its edges is doubled?

© 1994-2005 The Math Forum; http://mathforum.org/pow/

SOLUTION TO GRADE 6 PROBLEM-SOLVING TASK

The surface area of the new cube is 96 square cm. The volume of the new cube is 64 cubic cm. The surface area of the doubled edge cube is 4 times the original cube's surface area. The volume of the doubled-edge cube is 8 times the original cube's volume.

Surface Area = Width $\times$ Length $\times$ 6

Volume = Width $\times$ Length $\times$ Depth

SA of 2 cm cube = $2 \times 2 \times 6 = 24$

V of 2 cm cube = $2 \times 2 \times 2 = 8$

SA of 4 cm cube = $(2 \times 2) \times (2 \times 2) \times 6 = 96$

V of 4 cm cube = $(2 \times 2) \times (2 \times 2) \times (2 \times 2) = 64$

SA of 8 cm cube = $(2 \times 4) \times (2 \times 4) \times 6 = 384$

V of 4 cm cube = $(2 \times 4) \times (2 \times 4) \times (2 \times 4) = 512$

When we double the edge, the surface area is 4 times the surface area of the original cube, and the volume is 8 times the original size.

SA of edge $\times$ 2 = $(2 \times edge) \times (2 \times edge) \times 6$

$= 2 \times 2 \times edge \times edge \times 6$

$= 4 \times original\ SA$

V of edge $\times$ 2 cube = $(2 \times edge) \times (2 \times edge) \times (2 \times edge) =$ $2 \times 2 \times 2 \times edge \times edge \times edge = 8 \times original\ volume$

Step 3: Sixth-Grade Conceptual Understanding

The following is a sample Conceptual Understanding Unit matched to the strand or standard of *geometry*. It was selected to align with the Problem-Solving Task shown in step 2.

Grade Level: 6

Conceptual Unit Focus: Geometry

Standards and Indicators Matched to Unit Focus:
[Here teachers list and "unwrap" the full text of the relevant standard and indicators from individual district or state documents for the selected topic. *Source:* California Math Standards, Grade 6, 1.0, 2.0.]

"Unwrapped" Concepts: Need to Know about Geometry and Spatial Sense

- ❏ Two-dimensional figures
- ❏ Three-dimensional figures
- ❏ Interior angle measures
- ❏ Congruent angles/sides
- ❏ Geometry vocabulary:
  - ○ Altitude
  - ○ Diagonal
  - ○ Face
  - ○ Vertex
  - ○ All other polygons as listed below
- ❏ Polygons:
  - ○ Triangle
    - ◇ Acute
    - ◇ Obtuse

◇ Right

◇ Equilateral

○ Quadrilateral

◇ Square

◇ Rectangle

◇ Parallelogram

◇ Rhombus

◇ Trapezoid

○ Pentagon

○ Hexagon

○ Octagon

Skills: Be Able to Do:

❑ Classify (figures)

❑ Describe/predict (figures, sizes, positions, orientations)

❑ Use (proper language, classifications)

❑ Define (geometry vocabulary)

❑ Build (three-dimensional objects)

Topics or Context:

❑ Mathematics textbook

❑ Other resource materials (to be decided by teachers)

Big Ideas:

1. One-, two-, and three-dimensional figures have unique attributes.

2. Angles and sides have different measurements.

3. Different polygons have different measures of sides and angles.

4. Lines have perpendicular and parallel relationships.

Essential Questions:

1. What do you know about one-, two-, and three-dimensional figures?

Step 3: Sixth-Grade Conceptual Understanding

2. How are sides and angles described and measured?

3. What do you know about the attributes of polygons in terms of angles and sides?

4. How would you describe the relationships between lines on two- and three-dimensional figures?

End-of-Unit Assessment: "Geometry Box Project"

Using a shoebox, students will complete the following:

Side 1:

- Show pictures of listed triangles.
- Label each triangle.
- Write area and perimeter formulas for triangles.
- Write sentences about angles within shapes.

Side 2:

- Show pictures of listed quadrilaterals.
- Label each quadrilateral.
- Write area and perimeter formulas for each quadrilateral.
- Write sentences about angles within shapes.

Side 3:

- Measure the dimensions of the shoebox using centimeters.
- Write sentences about the relationship between lines on the shoebox.

Side 4:

- Using measurements from step 3, determine the surface area of the shoebox.
- Provide a written explanation of the method used to find the surface area.

Top and Bottom:

- Include student identifying information.

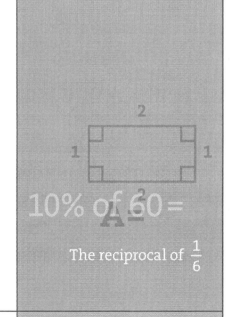

$$10\% \text{ of } 60 =$$

The reciprocal of $\frac{1}{6}$

Scoring Guide:

Exemplary:

- ❑ All "Proficient" criteria *plus*:
- ❑ Surface-area explanation is mathematically correct
- ❑ Sentences about angles show understanding of interior measure of polygons
- ❑ Sentences about lines indicate understanding of parallel and perpendicular

Proficient:

- ❑ Triangles listed correctly
- ❑ Quadrilaterals listed correctly
- ❑ Correct area and perimeter formulas
- ❑ Correct surface-area calculation

Progressing:

- ❑ Student work meets 3 of the "Proficient" criteria

Beginning:

- ❑ Student work meets fewer than 3 of the "Proficient" criteria
- ❑ Assessment task to be repeated after remediation

Peer's Evaluation (Optional) _____

Self-Evaluation _____

Teacher's Evaluation _____

Source: Adapted from work of Mrs. Kuhlke [school, district, and state unknown].

Step 4: Sixth-Grade Mastery of Math Facts

An effective way to practice math facts is through the processing of Math Review and by involving students in daily Mental Math activities. Sixth-grade students should continue development of their number sense by receiving regular practice with the number-sense patterns and math-fact patterns developed in grades 3 through 5. These patterns include:

Part-part-whole relationship for addition

"Think addition" for subtraction

Counting by a given number

Patterns within multiplication facts

"Think multiplication" for division

In addition, sixth-graders should extend and reinforce their math-fact strategies by applying them to multidigit problems. Instructional emphasis should be placed on the ability to use number sense to develop a reasonable answer before starting a computational procedure.

To assist sixth-grade students who are still struggling with their math facts, please refer again to Chapter 4 and the "Reproducibles" section at the end of this book for recommended strategies and other tips to differentiate instruction.

Step 5: Common Formative Assessment

As described in Chapter 5, common formative assessments administered to all students in the grade level can be identical or very similar in design to the end-of-unit classroom assessment. The grade-level, course, or department team of teachers that has already collaboratively designed a conceptual unit assessment for a key mathematical topic can simply use a similar assessment as the common formative assessment. However, whereas the classroom end-of-unit assessment is typically more performance-based (a Problem-Solving Task), the common formative assessment may also include computation problems or a blend of selected-response and constructed-response items.

Common formative assessments may also address standards other than those targeted during any one particular conceptual unit. Nevertheless, it is important to emphasize that common formative assessments are primarily designed to evaluate student proficiency on the math Power Standards *only*. Because there are so many variables to take into consideration when designing a common formative math assessment, we chose not to include a grade-level sample matched only to the particular math focus topic represented in steps 2 and 3.

Decisions as to the design, administration, scoring, analysis, and frequency of common formative assessments, to measure ongoing student understanding of particular math Power Standards, are left to the collaborative team of teachers. For guidelines in this regard, please refer again to Chapter 5.

Inside the Grade 7 and Grade 8 Classrooms

CHAPTER 7

In this chapter, we show the application of the five steps of the balanced math program model in either a grade 7 or a grade 8 classroom. The examples provided illustrate Math Review, Mental Math, problem solving, and a Conceptual Understanding Unit. In addition, we have included information regarding the teaching of math facts, even though we recognize that mastery of math facts is an elementary school responsibility. We hope these grade-specific examples will benefit middle school teachers in implementing these important balanced math program steps!

Step 1: Seventh- and Eighth-Grade Computational Skills (Math Review and Mental Math)

The Math Review Template

Math Review, as described in Chapter 1, occurs daily at the beginning of the math period. Seventh- and eighth-graders complete the five problems independently using paper and pencil. However, teachers will certainly need to make whatever modifications are necessary to ensure that students can be successful working on their own.

Using the Math Review template, teachers either write the problems on the board for students to copy or prepare an individual worksheet for each student.

1. $3.67 \times 10^4 =$ _____

Scientific Notation

2. The temperature increases from 80° to 100°. What is the percent of increase?

Percent

3. $4^3 \times 4^2 =$ _____

Exponents

4. Write an expression: The square of "a" is increased by the sum of twice "a" and 3.

Algebra Unit

5. Find area:

8″
12″

Geometry

6.

Bonus

PROCESSING SEQUENCE.

In this section are suggested strategies teachers can emphasize, during the processing of Math Review problems, to develop students' number sense and mathematical reasoning. Teachers can refer to these processing examples when developing their own strategies for processing Math Review problems. To complete Math Review within the allotted time frame, however, we suggest fully processing only two or three different problems each day. Provide just the answers for the others. There is not enough time to use every processing strategy for every problem every day, but do be sure to include *all* of these processing strategies over the course of each week. For the bonus problem, ask those students who solved it to orally state their answer along with a brief description of how they solved it.

**Step 1: Seventh- and Eighth-Grade Computational Skills
(Math Review and Mental Math)**

1. For the **Scientific Notation** problem:

   - The correct answer is 36,700

   - Ask students the purpose of scientific notation (an efficient and accurate method of writing very large or very small numbers)

   - Ask students what 10^4 equals (10,000)

   - Ask what happens when 3.67 is multiplied by 10; by 100; by 1,000

   - Ask what effect multiplying by powers of 10 has on the placement of the decimal

2. For the **Percent** problem:

   - The answer is 25%

   - Ask students what "percent of increase" means (the amount something increased from its starting point)

   - Ask where the temperature was in the beginning

   - Ask how much the temperature increased (20°)

   - Ask, "Assume that the temperature increased by 40°. What would be the percent of increase?" ($\frac{40}{80}$ = 50%)

   - Ask, "Assume that the temperature increased by 80°. What would be the percent of increase?" ($\frac{80}{80}$ = 100%)

   - Demonstrate a procedural method for solving the problem ($\frac{20}{80} = \frac{x}{100}$)

3. For the **Exponents** problem:

   - The product is 4^5

   - Ask students what $4^3 \times 4^2$ means

   - Emphasize correct use of vocabulary (4 is the base number; 3 is the exponent)

- Ask students to expand each power ($4^3 = 4 \times 4 \times 4$; $4^2 = 4 \times 4$)

- Ask students if they can state a generalization about exponents from this problem (when there is a common base number, add the exponents)

4. For the **Algebra Unit** problem:

- The answer is $a^2 + (2a + 3)$

- Ask students which words are important in the problem phrase (*square, increased by, sum, twice*)

- Ask which parts seem difficult

- Ask students to share their phrases and reasoning

- Listen for language issues that are creating confusion ("the sum of twice '*a*' and three" can be confusing)

- Ask if the expression will have an equals sign

- Agree upon a correct phrase as a class

5. For the **Geometry** problem:

- The answer is 48 in.^{2}

- Ask students to define *area*

- Ask what type of unit is used to express area (square units) and why (measure of covering)

- Ask what a square inch looks like

- Ask students if they know the formula for finding the area of a triangle

- Ask why the triangle is one-half the base multiplied by height (triangle is half a rectangular area with the same dimensions)

- Ask why the formula $\frac{1}{2} b + h$ works (perpendicular relationship of base and height creates square units)

Step 1: Seventh- and Eighth-Grade Computational Skills (Math Review and Mental Math)

The Math Review Quiz

The Math Review Quiz becomes a biweekly assessment of students' computational understanding. Its purpose is to assess students on a regular basis to determine their proficiency with the types of problems they are practicing daily during Math Review. Note that there are *two* problems for each type of daily problem the students have been practicing throughout the week.

1. $4.38 \times 10^3 =$ _____

2. $6.28 \times 10^4 =$ _____

3. The price of a cell phone increases from \$40 to \$50. What is the percent of increase?

4. The temperature increases from 50° to 90°. What is the percent of increase?

5. $5^3 \times 5^4 =$ _____

6. $7^2 \times 7^3 =$ _____

7. Write an expression: The product of 3 and "*a*" is decreased by the quotient of "*a*" divided by 4.

8. Write an expression: The sum of "*a*" and 4 is increased by the product of "*a*" and 6.

9. Find area: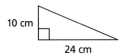
   10 cm
   24 cm

10. Find area: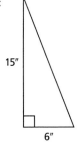
    15"
    6"

 (10 cm, 24 cm triangle)

 (15", 6" triangle)

Mental Math should be matched to the content of Math Review. Regular practice will help develop students' number sense.

Mental Math

Mental Math should be matched to the content of Math Review. Regular practice will help develop students' number sense. Here are three examples of Mental Math problems that are appropriate for grades 7 and 8, with incremental answers provided. The word "equals" signals students to say or write the answer (provided in the last parenthetical of the problem in each of the following examples). Note also the Mental Math themes for each particular type of problem. Seventh- and eighth-grade teachers may use these examples as guidelines for developing their own Mental Math problems.

EXAMPLES

"$\frac{3}{4}$ of 20 **(15)**; $\frac{1}{3}$ of the answer **(5)**; multiply the answer by 8 **(40)**; $\frac{3}{5}$ of the answer **(24)**; $\frac{1}{3}$ of the answer **(8)**; $\frac{1}{2}$ of the answer **(4)**; $\frac{1}{4}$ of the answer **(1)**; equals _____ ."
(Theme: fractional parts of a whole)

"2^3 **(8)**; square the answer **(64)**; add 36 **(100)**; take the square root of the answer **(10)**; take the answer to the fourth power **(10,000)**; equals _____ ."
(Theme: exponents)

"Start with the number of centimeters in 2 meters **(200)**; multiply by the number of ounces in a cup **(1,600)**; divide the answer by 4^2 **(100)**; multiply by the number of quarts in a gallon **(400)**; equals _____ ."
(Theme: measurement)

Step 2: Seventh- and Eighth-Grade Problem Solving

Sample Grades 7 and 8 Problem-Solving Task

The following is a sample Problem-Solving Task from the Website of the Math Forum @ Drexel (http://mathforum.org/pow/), an excellent problem-solving resource for teachers. The Forum's Problem of the Week service provides challenging, nonroutine word problems for students to solve online in a mentored environment. This particular problem is matched to the strand or standard of *algebra*. It was selected to align with the Conceptual Understanding Unit shown in step 3 (see next section). A student solution to the task appears after the problem. Readers may want to solve the problem themselves before taking a look at the solution. These problems can be quite challenging!

MATH FORUM PROBLEM-SOLVING TASK

2944: Power-full Fractions

At the start of the school year, Ms. Zhong likes to present her algebra class with a challenging problem that reviews many of the things they have learned so far about numbers. This year she wrote the following expression on the chalk board:

$$\left(\frac{A}{B}\right)^C + \left(\frac{D}{E}\right)^F + \left(\frac{G}{H}\right)^I$$

Then she turned to the class and said, "In this expression you are to replace the variables with the digits from 1 to 9, using each digit exactly once. Then find the expression's simplified value. Your objective is to substitute in such a way that the value turns out to be an integer, that is, a whole number."

By the end of the week the class had found quite a long list of integral values.

1. Find three possible solutions to Ms. Zhong's challenge.

2. What do you think is the largest value they could have found?

3. What do you think the smallest could be?

Extra: Can you figure out how many possibilities there are? (You don't have to actually find all of the answers.)

Note: When typing your answer, you can use the character ^ to indicate that the next item is an exponent.

SOLUTION TO GRADES 7 AND 8 PROBLEM-SOLVING TASK.

Three possible solutions to this problem are 672, 2,432, and 134,217,888. The largest possible solution is 134,217,888 and the smallest possible solution is 374.

The first step in solving this problem is to look for how to make the answer come out as an integer. The most obvious way to do this is if $(\frac{A}{B})$, $(\frac{D}{E})$, and $(\frac{G}{H})$ are integers. This means that A is a multiple of B, D is a multiple of E, and G is a multiple of H.

Next, I listed fractions in which the numerator is a multiple of the denominator. They are listed below:

$$\frac{2}{1} \quad \frac{3}{1} \quad \frac{4}{1} \quad \frac{5}{1} \quad \frac{6}{1} \quad \frac{7}{1} \quad \frac{8}{1} \quad \frac{9}{1}$$

$$\frac{4}{2} \quad \frac{6}{2} \quad \frac{8}{2} \quad \frac{6}{3} \quad \frac{9}{3} \quad \frac{8}{4}$$

To find a solution to the problem, you must pick 3 of these fractions for the 3 fractions in the expression.

They cannot share a common number. Then, plug in the remaining 3 numbers for C, F, and I. The resulting expression will simplify to an integer.

Three of the many possible solutions to this problem are:

A = 2 B = 1 C = 5 D = 6 E = 3 F = 7 G = 8 H = 4 I = 9

Result = 672

A = 8 B = 1 C = 9 D = 6 E = 3 F = 7 G = 4 H = 2 I = 5

Result = 134,217,888

A = 8 B = 4 C = 1 D = 9 E = 3 F = 5 G = 6 H = 2 I = 7

Result = 2,432

The largest value you can get is 134,217,888.

You can get this if

A = 8 B = 1 C = 9 D = 6 E = 3 F = 7 G = 4 H = 2 I = 5.

Result = 134,217,888

The first step I took to find this was to see what is the biggest number I can get by using the integers from 1–9 in the expression $(\frac{A}{B})^C$. I came up with $(\frac{8}{1})^9$, (8^9) which simplifies to 134,217,728. So A = 8, B = 1, and C = 9.

Now, we have to pick from the remaining 6 numbers: 2, 3, 4, 5, 6, and 7. The three possible fractions you can make with those numbers (such that the result will be an integer) are $\frac{6}{2}$, $\frac{6}{3}$, and $\frac{4}{2}$. You have to pick 2 of those so that they don't share a common number. The only way you can do that is if you use $\frac{6}{3}$ and $\frac{4}{2}$. So, D = 6, E = 3, G = 4, and H = 2.

Now, the only numbers left are 5 and 7. You have to choose which one is the exponent for which fraction. Since both fractions ($\frac{6}{3}$ and $\frac{4}{2}$) are equal to 2, it doesn't matter which you use for which. So, I just assigned 7 as the exponent of ($\frac{6}{3}$) and 5 as the exponent of ($\frac{4}{2}$).

Step 3: Seventh- and Eighth-Grade Conceptual Understanding

The following is a sample Conceptual Understanding Unit matched to the strand or standard of *algebra*. It was selected to align with the Problem-Solving Task shown in step 2.

Grade Level: 7–8

Conceptual Unit Focus: Algebra

Standards and Indicators Matched to Unit Focus:
[Here teachers list and "unwrap" the full text of the relevant standard and indicators from individual district or state documents for the selected topic. *Source:* Ohio Standards: Patterns, Functions, and Algebra; Standard 4, Indicators 1–11.]

"Unwrapped" Concepts: Need to Know about Solving Linear Equations

- ❏ Standards 4.1, 4.5:
    - ○ Tables
    - ○ Graphs
    - ○ Linear equations
- ❏ Standard 4.10:
    - ○ Linear/nonlinear relationships
- ❏ Standards 4.7, 4.9:
    - ○ Simplified expressions
    - ○ Uses for variables
- ❏ Standards 4.3, 4.10:
    - ○ Linear/nonlinear progressions
    - ○ Change in variables

Skills: Be Able to <u>Do</u>:

- ❏ Represent (tables, rules, functions, patterns, graphs, expressions, linear equations, inequalities, number line, coordinate plane)
- ❏ Analyze (patterns, rules, functions, tables, graphs, expressions, relationships, linear and nonlinear changes)
- ❏ Recognize (uses for variables, simplified expressions)
- ❏ Explain (linear and nonlinear progressions, changes in variables)

Topics or Context:

- ❏ Use of patterns, functions, and algebraic expressions in a variety of problem-solving situations

Big Ideas:

1. Tables, graphs, and equations provide a variety of ways to solve the same problem.

2. Variables are used to generalize patterns and can be simplified to make equivalent expressions.

3. Algebra can be used to explain linear and nonlinear progressions.

4. Substituting values into equations changes the output.

5. Formulas provide a systematic method for problem solving.

Essential Questions:

1. How can you solve algebraic problems? Explain another method to solve the same problem.

2. How can you tell if two expressions are equivalent?

3. How are linear and nonlinear equations similar and different?

4. Why can the same equation give us several different answers?

5. How are formulas helpful?

Step 3: Seventh- and Eighth-Grade Conceptual Understanding

End-of-Unit Assessment: "Convince Your Parents to Help You Buy a Car"

Students will use the Internet to research the cost of a car based on parameters discussed in class. They will document the resources used. Next, they will develop a linear equation based on the predicted monthly payment, total cost of car, and down payment. Then, they will create a table, graph, and equation to display their research. Using the research collected, students will develop a sales presentation to convince their parents that they can save enough money in the next four years to pay for half of their dream car.

Scoring Guide:

Exemplary:

❏ All "Proficient" criteria *plus*:

❏ Presentation uses mathematics to build a convincing case

❏ Income table includes 3 or more entries

❏ Written explanation shows how table, graph, and equation solve the problem

Proficient:

❏ Income table has at least two entries

❏ Correct equation with explanation of meaning for numbers and variables

❏ Table, graph, and equation all show solution to problem

❏ Presentation is completed according to assignment requirements

Progressing:

❏ Student work meets 3 of the "Proficient" criteria

Beginning:

❏ Student work meets fewer than 3 of the "Proficient" criteria

❏ Assessment task to be repeated after remediation

Peer's Evaluation (Optional) _____

Self-Evaluation _____

Teacher's Evaluation _____

Source: Katie Wentworth and Sarah Martin, Oakwood City Schools, Dayton, OH.

Step 4: Seventh- and Eighth-Grade Mastery of Math Facts

An effective way to practice math facts is through the processing of Math Review and by involving students in daily Mental Math activities. To solve multidigit problems with various operations, seventh- and eighth-grade students should continue to extend and apply the number sense and basic math-fact strategies developed in elementary grades.

To assist seventh- and eighth-grade students who are still struggling with their math facts, please refer again to Chapter 4 and the "Reproducibles" section at the end of this book for recommended strategies and other tips to differentiate instruction.

Step 5: Common Formative Assessment

As described in Chapter 5, common formative assessments administered to all students in the grade level, course, or department can be identical or very similar in design to the end-of-unit classroom assessment. The grade-level team of teachers that has already collaboratively designed a conceptual unit assessment for a key mathematical topic can simply use a similar assessment as the common formative assessment. However, whereas the classroom end-of-unit assessment is typically more performance-based (a Problem-Solving Task), the common formative assessment may additionally include computation problems or a blend of selected-response and constructed-response items.

Common formative assessments may also address standards other than those targeted during any one particular conceptual unit. Nevertheless, it is important to emphasize that common formative assessments are primarily designed to evaluate student proficiency of the math Power Standards *only*. Because there are so many variables to take into consideration when designing a common formative math assessment, we chose not to include a grade-level sample matched only to the particular math focus topic represented in steps 2 and 3.

Decisions as to the design, administration, scoring, analysis, and frequency of common formative assessments, to measure ongoing student understanding of particular math Power Standards, are left to the collaborative team of teachers. For guidelines in this regard, please refer again to Chapter 5.

Inside the High School Classroom

CHAPTER 8

In this chapter, we show the application of the five steps of the balanced math program model in the high school classroom. The examples provided illustrate Math Review, Mental Math, problem solving, and a Conceptual Understanding Unit. In addition, we have included information regarding the teaching of math facts, even though we recognize that mastery of math facts is an elementary school responsibility. We hope these grade-specific examples will benefit high school teachers in implementing these important balanced math program steps!

Step 1: Computational Skills (Math Review and Mental Math) for Grades 9 and 10

The Math Review Template

Math Review, as described in Chapter 1, occurs daily at the beginning of the math period. Ninth- and tenth-graders in Algebra I complete the five problems independently using paper and pencil. However, teachers will certainly need to make whatever modifications are necessary to ensure that students can be successful working on their own.

Using the Math Review template, teachers either write the problems on the board for students to copy or prepare an individual worksheet for each student.

1. Convert each fraction to decimal and to percent.

$\frac{1}{3} = $ _____ $= $ _____

$\frac{2}{5} = $ _____ $= $ _____

$\frac{7}{8} = $ _____ $= $ _____

Fraction/Decimal/ Percent

2. $-4 + 6 + 7 - (-4) + 12 = $ _____

Integers

3. $2^3 + 4^{-2} + 2 = $ _____

Exponents

4. Solve using proportion: If 2 gallons of paint cover 900 sq. ft., how many gallons are needed to paint 2,520 sq. ft.?

Ratio/Proportion

5. Solve for x.

Geometry (Pythagorean Theorem)

6.

Bonus

PROCESSING SEQUENCE.

In this section are suggested strategies teachers can emphasize, during the processing of Math Review problems, to develop students' number sense and mathematical reasoning. Teachers can refer to these processing examples when developing their own strategies for processing Math Review problems. To complete Math Review within the allotted time frame, however, we suggest fully processing only two or three different problems each day. Provide just the answers for the others. There is not enough time to use every processing strategy for every problem every day, but do be sure to include *all* of these processing strategies over the course of each week. For the bonus problem, ask those students who

solved it to orally state their answer along with a brief description
of how they solved it.

1. For the **Fraction/Decimal/Percent** problem:

    *   The correct answers are $\frac{1}{3} = .33 = 33\frac{1}{3}\%$; $\frac{2}{5} = .40 = 40\%$;
        $\frac{7}{8} = .875 = 87.5\%$

    *   Ask students to share their methods for conversion (pattern
        within fraction—if you know $\frac{1}{8}$, you can find $\frac{7}{8}$ easily)

    *   Ask students to consider relative size of the fraction by
        comparing to $\frac{1}{2}$ ($\frac{2}{5} < \frac{1}{2}$; $\frac{7}{8} > \frac{1}{2}$) and to one whole ($\frac{7}{8}$ is close
        to a whole)

    *   Demonstrate procedural method

2. For the **Integers** problem:

    *   The correct answer is 25

    *   Ask students which operations are confusing

    *   Ask students to share their strategies for the operations

    *   Have students share different ways to group the integers
        to find the answer

    *   Remind students about rules for integer operations

3. For the **Exponents** problem:

    *   The correct answer is $10\frac{1}{16}$

    *   Ask students what they know about negative exponents

    *   Show pattern that demonstrates what happens with
        negative exponents ($2^4 = 16$; $2^3 = 8$; $2^2 = 4$; $2^1 = 2$; $2^0 = 1$;
        $2^{-1} = \frac{1}{2}$; $2^{-2} = \frac{1}{4}$; $2^{-3} = \frac{1}{8}$; and so on. The pattern is that each
        product decreases by half. This pattern also demonstrates
        why negative exponents produce fractional answers that
        also continue to decrease by half as the pattern continues.)

- Ask students to develop a reasonable answer (greater than 2)

- Demonstrate a procedural method used to solve the problem

4. For the **Ratio/Proportion** problem:

- The correct answer is 5.6 gallons

- Ask students to develop a reasonable answer (1 gallon covers 450 sq. ft.;

  $450 \times$ _____ $= 2,520$; approximately 6 gallons)

- Have students share their strategies to develop a reasonable answer

- Ask students for a definition of *ratio*

- Ask what ratio is supplied in the problem (2 gallons/900 sq. ft.)

- Demonstrate proportion process

5. For the **Geometry** problem:

- The answer is 15

- Ask students what they know about right triangles

- Ask what students know about the relationship between the sides ($a^2 + b^2 = c^2$)

- Ask what they know about the hypotenuse (longest side because it is across from the largest angle)

- Have students develop a reasonable answer (less than 17; smaller than hypotenuse)

- Ask if students know a triple that relates to the problem (8, 15, and 17)

- Demonstrate mathematical procedure ($8^2 + x^2 = 17^2$)

The Math Review Quiz

The Math Review Quiz becomes a biweekly assessment of students' computational understanding. Its purpose is to assess students on a regular basis to determine their proficiency with the types of problems they are practicing daily during Math Review. Note that there are *two* problems for each type of daily problem the students have been practicing throughout the week.

1. Convert to decimal and percent:

    $\frac{2}{3} =$ _____ $=$ _____ ; $\frac{3}{5} =$ _____ $=$ _____

2. Convert to decimal and percent:

    $\frac{3}{8} =$ _____ $=$ _____ ; $\frac{5}{8} =$ _____ $=$ _____

3. $-6 + (-7) - (-5) + 8 =$ _____

4. $\dfrac{(-2) \times (-4) \times (5) \times (-12)}{-20} =$ _____

5. $4^{-3} + 2^{-3} + 8 =$ _____

6. $\dfrac{5^4 \times 4^3 \times 2^5}{5^2 \times 4^5 \times 2} =$ _____

7. Solve using proportion: If a hose fills up a 5-gallon bucket in 4 minutes, how many minutes will it take to fill up an 18-gallon bucket?

8. Solve using proportion: If a gardener can mow two lawns in three hours, how many hours will it take the gardener to mow nine lawns?

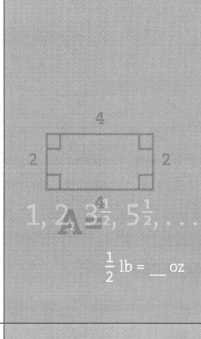

9. Solve for the missing side:

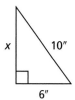

12 cm   *x*

5 cm

10. Solve for the missing side:

x   10″

6″

Mental Math

Mental Math should be matched to the content of Math Review. Regular practice will help develop students' number sense. Here are three examples of Mental Math problems that are appropriate for high school, with incremental answers provided. The word "equals" signals students to say or write the answer (provided in the last parenthetical of the problem in each of the following examples). Note also the Mental Math themes for each particular type of problem. High school teachers may use these examples as guidelines for developing their own Mental Math problems.

EXAMPLES

"4^2 **(16)**; add 20 **(36)**; square root of answer **(6)**; cube the answer **(216)**; add 9 **(225)**; square root of answer **(15)**; multiply by 10 **(150)**; subtract 6 **(144)**; square root of answer **(12)**; equals _____ ." *(Theme: square roots)*

Step 2: High School Problem Solving

"$\frac{3}{5}$ of 20 (12); plus 75% of answer (21); $\frac{3}{7}$ of answer (9); $\frac{2}{3}$ of answer (6); square the answer (36); add 4 (40); 40% of the answer (16); equals _____ ."

(Theme: fractional parts of a quantity)

"$-2 + 4$ (2); multiply by -10 (-20); divide by 4 (-5); subtract -7 (-12); square the answer (144); add -4 (140); divide by -7 (-20); equals _____ ."

(Theme: integers)

Step 2: High School Problem Solving

Sample High School Problem-Solving Task

The following is a sample Problem-Solving Task from the Website of the Math Forum @ Drexel (http://mathforum.org/pow/), an excellent problem-solving resource for teachers. The Forum's Problem of the Week service provides challenging, nonroutine word problems for students to solve online in a mentored environment. This particular problem is matched to the strand or standard of *geometry*. It was selected to align with the Conceptual Understanding Unit shown in step 3 (see next section). A student solution to the task appears after the problem. Readers may want to solve the problem themselves before taking a look at the solution. These problems can be quite challenging!

MATH FORUM PROBLEM-SOLVING TASK

1107: Equilateral Triangles and Circles

Two vertices of an equilateral triangle are on the diameter of a circle. The other vertex of the triangle is on the circumference of the circle. If the area of the circle is 49 pi units^2, what's the largest possible area of the triangle?

Bonus: If all three vertices of the triangle are on the circle, what's the area of the triangle?

© 1994-2005 The Math Forum; http://mathforum.org/pow/

SOLUTION TO HIGH SCHOOL PROBLEM-SOLVING TASK.

The area of the triangle is (49 * square root of 3) over 3. The first thing that I assumed is that if it was going to be the largest possible triangle, the vertices on the diameter must be on the diameter's endpoints. But then I remembered that an inscribed triangle with vertices on the endpoints of the diameter makes a 90-degree angle, and that, of course, does not make an equilateral triangle.

Then I decided to drop an altitude to form two 30-60-90 triangles. The altitude's length is 7, because if the area is 49 pi units squared and the area of a circle is pi * radius squared, all I had to do was find the square root of 49 (7).

Next, I used the special rules governing a 30-60-90 triangle, and to go from the altitude to the base I could just divide by the square root of 3. This gave me a height of 7 and a base of (7/sq. root of 3 + 7/sq. root of 3). I got rid of the radicals by multiplying both by sq. root of 3/sq. root of 3.

> This left me with (14 * sq. root of 3)/3 as the base and 7 was still the height. I plugged these into the area formula (1/2 * b * h, or bh/2), bh = (98 * sq. root of 3)/3, then I multiplied by 1/2: (98 * sq. root of 3)/6. Simplified, it became 49 * sq. root of 3)/3.

Step 3: High School Conceptual Understanding

The following is a sample Conceptual Understanding Unit matched to the strand or standard of *geometry*. It was selected to align with the Problem-Solving Task shown in step 2.

Grade Level: High school

Conceptual Unit Focus: Geometry

Standards and Indicators Matched to Unit Focus:
[Here teachers list and "unwrap" the full text of the relevant standard and indicators from individual district or state documents for the selected topic. *Source:* Indiana Geometry Standard 6, Indicators 6.7, 2.5, 3.3, 4.4.]

"Unwrapped" Concepts: Need to Know about <u>Geometry</u>
- ❑ Circle:
    - ○ Area
    - ○ Circumference
    - ○ Arc Length
- ❑ Area:
    - ○ Sector
    - ○ Polygons
- ❑ Probability

Skills: Be Able to Do:

- ❏ Compute (circumference, area)
- ❏ Find (probability of a region of a circle)
- ❏ Use (area of polygons)
- ❏ Define (area of sectors)

Topics or Context:

- ❏ Text lessons 11.4, 11.5, and 11.6. Provide activities for finding regular polygonal areas, circumference, arc length, circle area, sector area, and areas of regions bounded by circles and regular polygons. These lessons are included in a multiweek differentiated unit on circles.

Big Ideas:

1. Circles and regions of circles are designs used in business, art, and life.

2. Computing circle area and circumference, arc length, sector areas, and regional areas is a process combining prescribed formulas and commonsense applications.

3. Games involving probability based on pictures or design are a component of geometric area and probability.

Essential Questions:

1. How is understanding the area of circles and regions bounded by circles and polygons necessary in art and life? (addresses both the first and second Big Ideas of this unit)

2. How is geometric probability used in the creation of some games?

Step 3: High School Conceptual Understanding

End-of-Unit Assessment: "Geometry: It's Fair Game"

Students will design and create a board game using geometric design and probability as the key components of the game. They will draw or construct a design of the game composed of circles and regular polygons. They will then create the rules of the game and explain them in detail. Next, they will compute and report the area of each region on the board and compute the probability of landing on each region. Finally, the students will write about how they designed their game and their understanding of circles and probability.

Scoring Guide:

Exemplary:

❑ All "Proficient" criteria *plus*:

❑ Process of how to win the game is explained with supporting examples

❑ Written explanation demonstrates understanding of circles and probability

Proficient:

❑ Game board includes circles and regular polygons

❑ Values and probability of success are marked on game board

❑ Game and rules are explained in detail

❑ Area and probability of each region are correctly computed

❑ Written explanation included

Progressing:

❑ Student work meets 4 of the "Proficient" criteria

Beginning:

❑ Student work meets fewer than 4 of the "Proficient" criteria

❑ Assessment task to be repeated after remediation

Peer's Evaluation (Optional) _____

Self-Evaluation _____

Teacher's Evaluation _____

Source: Adapted from work of Richard C. Fair, MSD of Wayne Township, Indianapolis, IN.

Step 4: High School Mastery of Math Facts

An effective way to practice math facts is through the processing of Math Review and by involving students in daily Mental Math activities.

To assist high school students who are still struggling with their math facts, please refer again to Chapter 4 and the "Reproducibles" section at the end of this book for recommended strategies and other tips to differentiate instruction.

Step 5: Common Formative Assessment

As described in Chapter 5, common formative assessments administered to all students in the grade level can be identical or very similar in design to the end-of-unit classroom assessment. The grade-level, course, or department team of teachers that has already collaboratively designed a conceptual unit assessment for a key mathematical topic can simply use a similar assessment as the common formative assessment. However, whereas the classroom end-of-unit assessment is typically more performance-based (a Problem-Solving Task), the common formative assessment may additionally include computation problems or a blend of selected-response and constructed-response items.

Common formative assessments may also address standards other than those targeted during any one particular conceptual unit. Nevertheless, it is important to emphasize that common formative assessments are primarily designed to evaluate student proficiency on the math Power Standards only. Because there are so many variables to take into consideration when designing a common formative math assessment, we chose not to include a grade-level or math course sample matched only to the particular math focus topic represented in steps 2 and 3.

Decisions as to the design, administration, scoring, analysis, and frequency of common formative assessments, to measure ongoing student understanding of particular math Power Standards, are left to the collaborative team of teachers. For guidelines in this regard, please refer again to Chapter 5.

PART THREE

Resources for Implementation

Putting It All Together: Time Management and Frequently Asked Questions

CHAPTER 9

So there you have it: the five steps to implementing a balanced math program! Even though it will certainly take time and perseverance to incorporate each of these steps into the math instruction and assessment practices of your school, the steps will become easier as teachers deepen their understanding of the program through firsthand experience.

This chapter is divided into two sections. In the first, we offer practical suggestions for time management that have proven effective. In the second, we share the questions most frequently asked by teachers during Five Easy Steps *workshops and provide the answers to address them.*

Part 1: Time Management

Regardless of whether one teaches a self-contained class of elementary-grade children or several sections of students in a secondary setting, classroom teachers face the uncompromising time constraints of the ever-ticking clock. An elementary teacher is responsible for teaching the standards in all the academic content areas, and must continually adjust the daily schedule to meet the demands of doing so. The time allotment for mathematics often varies according to the individual school or grade level and the number of instructional minutes mandated by the school district. As a general rule of thumb, however, elementary teachers devote about 60 to 75 minutes to math 5 days each week. Because they are typically with the same students all day, they can decide whether to schedule math in the morning or the afternoon.

> *We hope that you, as a secondary math teacher, are concluding your study of this book with new ideas for maximizing the time available for math instruction and assessment in your particular situation.*

A secondary-grade math teacher may have only one content area to focus on, but must strive to meet the needs of several sections of students, each within a fixed time frame of 54 minutes or less. Recognition of the need for more instructional time is one of the reasons why so many middle schools and high schools are moving to a block or modified block schedule. Still, the challenge is great for those who decide to incorporate computational practice, problem-solving experiences, and lessons that emphasize conceptual understanding (as described in Chapters 1, 2, and 3, respectively) within the preset time limits of each day's schedule.

We hope that you, as a secondary math teacher, are concluding your study of this book with new ideas for maximizing the time available for math instruction and assessment in your particular situation. The following is a suggested schedule for implementing the *Five Easy Steps* in a secondary-grade classroom following a traditional bell schedule.

Daily Math Schedule for Secondary Grades

Because the time allotment for a secondary-grade teacher is fixed, a conceptual unit may take longer to get through than it would in elementary school. For this reason, we have provided a daily math schedule that extends over a four-week period, rather than a three-week period. This allows the teacher to effectively incorporate Math Review and Mental Math (step 1); problem solving (step 2), once students can complete the process independently; and conceptual unit design (step 3). This sample schedule is based on a 54-minute period, but you can adjust it to equal the specific minutes in your own schedule. Although the weeks may look very similar, note the **bold** and *italicized* items indicating the particular changes needed to enable you to include all three steps.

Secondary Math Schedule
Week One

MONDAY

Math Review—15 minutes

Mental Math—5 minutes

Conceptual Understanding Unit lesson—34 minutes

TUESDAY

Math Review—15 minutes

Mental Math—5 minutes

Conceptual Understanding Unit lesson—34 minutes

Problem-Solving Task assigned (Data Sheet due on Friday)

WEDNESDAY

Math Review—15 minutes

Mental Math—5 minutes

Conceptual Understanding Unit lesson—34 minutes

THURSDAY

Math Review—15 minutes

Mental Math—5 minutes

Conceptual Understanding Unit lesson—34 minutes

FRIDAY

Math Review—15 minutes

Data Sheet discussion—35 minutes

Week Two

MONDAY

Math Review—15 minutes

Mental Math—5 minutes

Conceptual Understanding Unit lesson—34 minutes

TUESDAY

Math Review—15 minutes

Mental Math—5 minutes

Conceptual Understanding Unit lesson—34 minutes

Problem-Solving Task Write-Up due

WEDNESDAY

Process and peer-assess Problem-Solving Task problem—54 minutes

THURSDAY

Math Review—15 minutes

Mental Math—5 minutes

Conceptual Understanding Unit lesson—34 minutes

FRIDAY

Math Review Quiz; score quiz in class together—34 minutes

Conceptual Understanding Unit lesson—20 minutes

Week Three

MONDAY

Process Math Review Quiz (error analysis, self-reflection)—30 minutes

Conceptual Understanding Unit lesson—24 minutes

TUESDAY

Math Review—15 minutes

Mental Math—5 minutes

Conceptual Understanding Unit lesson—34 minutes

Assign Problem-Solving Task (Data Sheet due Friday)

WEDNESDAY

Math Review—15 minutes

Mental Math—5 minutes

Conceptual Understanding Unit lesson—34 minutes

THURSDAY

> **Math Review**—15 minutes
>
> **Mental Math**—5 minutes
>
> **Conceptual Understanding Unit lesson**—34 minutes

FRIDAY

> **Math Review**—15 minutes
>
> *Data Sheet discussion*—35 minutes

Week Four

MONDAY

> **Math Review**—15 minutes
>
> **Mental Math**—5 minutes
>
> **Conceptual Understanding Unit lesson**—34 minutes

TUESDAY

> **Math Review**—15 minutes
>
> **Mental Math**—5 minutes
>
> **Conceptual Understanding Unit lesson**—34 minutes
>
> *Problem-Solving Task Write-Up due*

WEDNESDAY

> *Process and peer-assess Problem-Solving Task*—54 minutes

THURSDAY

> **Math Review**—15 minutes
>
> **Mental Math**—5 minutes
>
> **Conceptual Understanding Unit lesson**—34 minutes

FRIDAY

> *Math Review Quiz; score quiz in class together*—34 minutes
>
> **Conceptual Understanding Unit lesson**—20 minutes

Part 2: Frequently Asked Questions

Following are the most frequently asked questions we receive from across the country during the *Five Easy Steps to a Balanced Math Program* workshops. Because these questions are relevant and applicable to primary, upper elementary, and secondary grades, we have included this section in all three editions of *Five Easy Steps to a Balanced Math Program*.

The responses to these questions have been organized according to each of the first four steps only. Readers interested in learning more about the implementation of step 5, Common Formative Assessment, are encouraged to refer to the published works on this topic, several of which are cited in Chapter 5.

Step 1: Computational Skills
(Math Review and Mental Math)

MATH REVIEW.

Q. *Do I need to do Math Review every day?*

A. The Math Review process is most successful if students complete it daily. Students need multiple opportunities to practice problems if they are to become proficient with self-diagnosis. The learning process must involve repeated reasoning and "shaping" opportunities that allow students to develop or "shape" their understanding about a particular concept or skill. Students learn by trying a skill, receiving feedback on that skill, shaping their understanding about that skill, and then trying the skill again. Typically, it takes 24 repetitions with a skill to reach 80% accuracy (Marzano, 2003, p. 67).

Part 2: Frequently Asked Questions

Q. *Is it necessary to do five problems every day?*

A. The number of problems can be adjusted according to the amount of classroom time allotted to math instruction. Five problems fit within most math instructional-minute models. It is important not to do more than five problems, because you do not want Math Review to take over your daily math program. Our experience shows that five problems allow the teacher to successfully address (and close!) the gaps in student understanding of computational skills.

Q. *Is it effective to organize math problems by type and work on only one type of problem per day?*

A. Organizing problems by type within the Math Review process and working on one type each day does not allow students the multiple opportunities they need to diagnose their misunderstandings and receive necessary feedback. As stated earlier, students need multiple opportunities to shape their understanding of a concept or skill. The *Five Easy Steps* process allows students to practice multiple skills for several days and to receive feedback on each of those skills every day, increasing the probability that students will actually understand and thus retain those skills.

Q. *Is it necessary to do the Math Review Quiz?*

A. The Math Review Quiz is essential to the Math Review process (beginning in grade 1). The Math Review Quiz gives the teacher the diagnostic information necessary to determine the effectiveness of instruction; more importantly, the quiz provides students with necessary feedback about their own degree of understanding. After practicing skills and then reflecting on those skills, students need the opportunity to check their level of understanding associated with a particular concept. The Math

Math Review is designed to review concepts and skills that students have already received instruction in and maintain them through additional practice. It is not a process for introducing new information.

Review Quiz also helps the teacher decide when it is time to change the particular type of problems that are being presented during Math Review.

Q. *Won't the processing of Math Review take forever?*

A. The processing methods described in this book will keep the process moving along. It does take self-discipline to keep the processing of the Math Review problems within a certain time frame, but this will become second nature after a couple of weeks.

Q. *Can I present new concepts during Math Review?*

A. Math Review is designed to *review* concepts and skills that students have already received instruction in and *maintain* them through additional practice. It is not a process for introducing new information. If Math Review is used to present formal instruction of new concepts, the timing structure presented in the book will not work.

Q. *What do I do with students who finish quickly?*

A. An effective means of differentiating Math Review is to present a daily bonus problem available to all students who finish the regular material early. This bonus problem should challenge students who feel successful with the skills presented in Math Review. Also, students who finish early are quite effective at, and greatly enjoy, providing peer assistance to other students.

Q. *Is it effective to make up all of the Math Review problems for the entire year at the beginning of the year?*

A. The Math Review process is specifically designed to help the students currently in your classroom. Also, it is a diagnostic process that the teacher uses to modify and adjust instruction to fit the needs of those students. Math Review is not intended to be a "covering the curriculum" process; it is one that should naturally unfold as students work to improve their understanding of essential mathematical skills and concepts. Therefore, it is better to create the Math Review problems as the year progresses to reflect the specific and changing instructional needs of your students.

Q. *Could grade-level teachers rotate the responsibility for writing the Math Review problems for the entire grade level?*

A. It is effective for grade-level teams of teachers to decide together on the skills and concepts to be emphasized at their particular grade level, but sharing the writing of Math Review problems is not recommended because the problems should match the instructional needs of each teacher's students.

Q. *How does Math Review fit with commercially produced math programs that include a spiral review?*

A. Commercially produced programs can be used as a resource for sample Math Review problems, but such programs often do not precisely fit the needs of your current students. The premise for conducting a spiral review is valid: if students practice a skill periodically over time, they will remember and be successful with that skill. Commercially produced programs usually do not include a process through which students can determine why they do not understand a particular skill or concept. Because the Math Review process emphasizes error analysis, teachers are better able to diagnose student learning needs and adjust instruction accordingly than they can when using a commercially produced program that requires them to adhere to a set pacing schedule with prescribed problems. Because students

> *It is better to create the Math Review problems as the year progresses to reflect the specific and changing instructional needs of your students.*

have regular opportunities to self-diagnose and identify their own particular misunderstandings during Math Review, they develop and retain correct mathematical understandings.

Q. *Should I collect and look through the Math Review papers daily?*

A. Daily collection and perusal of the Math Review papers provides the teacher with valuable diagnostic information about student understanding and student misconceptions. If classroom teachers incorporate the reflective part of the Math Review process, they will receive valuable information about student errors that they can then use to differentiate instruction.

Q. *I really don't have time to include the reflective piece, so is it okay to leave it out?*

A. The reflective piece helps students pinpoint their errors and determine why they do not understand a given skill or concept. It also encourages students to become responsible for their own learning by involving each student in the instructional process. Instead of students saying, "I got the wrong answer" or "I'm bad at math," self-reflection—based on error analysis— focuses students on what they *do* understand and reveals the particular part of a concept or skill that they do not yet understand.

MENTAL MATH.

Q. *Do I have to make up the Mental Math problems myself?*

A. Grade-level teams of teachers can make up Mental Math problems together. Also, there are commercially produced teacher support materials that have examples of Mental Math activities. Certain textbook series provide resources for Mental Math problems. Our recommendation is that you first try making up a few problems with a grade-level peer by referencing the sample Mental Math problems provided in this book and then practice creating them on your own. Before you know it, you will be quite comfortable with the process. You might even find it to be fun!

Q. *I seem to skip the Mental Math activity. Do you have any suggestions that will help me to do it on a regular basis?*

A. Regularity of practice is very important. Students need to know that it is going to happen. Mental Math is the type of activity that can be done at any time during the day. We recommend that it be done after Math Review, but there is no reason not to do it at the end of a class period, before going to lunch or recess, or before leaving for the day. Often teachers report that they are unable to do it immediately after the processing of the Math Review problems and so they schedule it whenever they can. Teachers from all over the country have confirmed what we found in our own classroom experience using Mental Math: students LOVE it and will remind you if you forget to include it!

Q. *What is the point of having a theme for Mental Math?*

A. A theme in Mental Math gives students repeated practice with patterns within the number system. A theme also provides the teacher with a method of emphasizing essential math concepts for the grade level. A good strategy is to ask students if they recognize the theme of the Mental Math problem presented.

Q. *Should I quiz students on Mental Math or give a grade for this activity?*

A. No. Mental Math is designed to be quick, informal, and fun. It is intended to be a tool for practice and development of number sense, not a tool for assessment. Mental Math provides students with an opportunity to explore different strategies involving numbers and to hear other students' strategies.

Q. *Are students capable of making up good problems?*

A. Students are very capable of making up good Mental Math problems. However, require them to make up the problem the night before they want to present it to the class, so that they (and you) have an opportunity to check its accuracy and practice saying the problem at an effective speed. Another effective technique is to distribute index cards to students who wish to present a Mental Math problem to the class. The student copies his or her problem on the card, writes his or her name on it, and submits the card to the teacher. Each day the teacher draws one of the submitted cards and that student then presents his or her problem to the class.

Allowing students to make up and present Mental Math problems is an excellent practice. Teachers gain valuable insights as to what their students understand and do not understand with regard to number sense.

Q. *How can I get all students to participate in Mental Math?
A few of my students just sit there while the other students are engaged in solving the given problem.*

A. The key is to create enough success and enthusiasm for Mental Math so that everyone wants to join in. Students who initially feel uncomfortable with the process need to experience success immediately so that they are motivated to try. Demonstrating a fun and enthusiastic attitude toward the activity can bring along the most reluctant of students.

Q. *How can I help my special-needs students become more successful with Mental Math? They have difficulty doing the problems in their heads at the same pace as the rest of the class, and often give up early or don't even try.*

A. To help these students succeed, allow them to use manipulatives or write down the answers incrementally as you progress through the Mental Math string of numbers and operations. Repeating the problem allows students who need assistance a second chance to arrive at the correct answer. Modeling this process with easier problems in the beginning will help support their ability to solve the problems independently. To help all students become successful, make whatever modifications you deem appropriate.

Q. *How do I determine the themes for Mental Math?*

A. The themes for Mental Math should be based on:

- Essential math standards or math Power Standards for the grade level

- Common student misunderstandings observed across the grade level

- Patterns within the number system

- General-knowledge information that students at the grade level should have

Mental Math themes can also focus on the development of and practice with basic math facts as appropriate for the particular grade level.

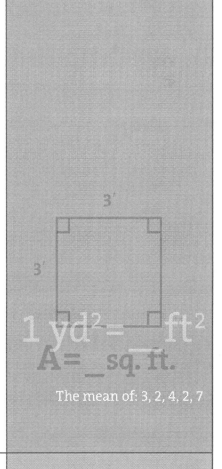

*Mental Math activities are
directly linked to the
concept of determining a
reasonable answer—an
essential skill for success
in mathematics.*

Q. *I'm not used to doing math in my head. How can I improve my own ability?*

A. Teachers—as well as students—will find that the more they do Mental Math, the more successful they become with it. Each time they practice, they are becoming more and more aware of number patterns and developing their own number sense. Our brains are amazing calculators if given the chance to prove it!

Q. *Mental Math seems fun, but how is it connected to being a successful math student?*

A. Mental Math activities allow students to develop effective strategies to use with number operations that they feel comfortable with and that are accurate and reliable for them. Mental Math activities are directly linked to the concept of determining a reasonable answer—an essential skill for success in mathematics. The Mental Math process also helps students become more effective test-takers. When students learn, through daily practice, the strategies of determining a reasonable answer and eliminating incorrect answer choices, they have gained a valuable skill.

Step 2: Problem Solving

Q. *I don't have time in my math program to do problem solving the way you recommend. Why is it valuable?*

A. Problem solving, as described in step 2, allows students the opportunity to apply the mathematics they have been learning. It emphasizes mathematical reasoning and the verbal and written explanation of student thinking—skills that are essential for success not only in school and on high-stakes state tests, but in life as well. Problem solving gives students opportunities to discuss mathematics with their peers and to have their mathematical thinking validated. Discussion and peer interaction are key components of learning mathematics effectively. The time this process takes is a tremendous investment in terms of the results gained.

Q. *What do I do about students who quickly get the answer in their heads but then can't explain their thinking?*

A. Providing both teacher and student models of mathematical explanations is very helpful for students who have a difficult time explaining their math processes. These students also benefit from multiple opportunities to revise their explanations. It is important to emphasize verification or proof of answers. Teachers who value reasoning, explanation, and verification as much as they do the correct answer will greatly help the student who says, "The answer just popped into my head." Such students will become successful at communicating *how* they determined their answers.

Q. *I have always disliked word problems. How can I help my students do problem solving when I myself am not very good at it?*

A. Even if you believe that you are not a "math person," it is important to develop the attitude that you can be successful with problem solving. An effective way to begin is to select problems with grade-level colleagues and solve the problems together before assigning the problems to your students. After solving the problems with your peers, solve the problem again, making sure you understand the mathematics presented in the problem. It is very important to be patient with yourself during this process. What you will find as you do the problems with students is that you are gaining insights from the students' reasoning. You will find that you are more of a math person than you thought!

Q. *My students resist problem solving. What do I do?*

A. Start with easy problems and help students experience immediate success. It is essential that you convince students that they are capable of doing problem solving. Use the whole-class approach described in Chapter 2 until you feel that students are gaining confidence as problem solvers. Older students who have not been successful with problem solving in earlier grades will be very resistant to problem solving in the beginning. It is essential that they feel there is hope for success.

Q. *How do I know if the Problem-Solving Task I have selected is a good one, and where do I find good problems?*

A. The most important criterion in selecting a Problem-Solving Task is that it matches the current math unit topic and that classroom instruction supports it. Students should not be asked to do a task that requires mathematics in which they have not received instruction. Determine whether the problem allows application of the mathematical ideas presented in the current instructional unit of study.

Other important criteria are that the problem be:

- At an appropriate difficulty level for students

- Accessible to all students

- Relevant, engaging, and challenging

- Approachable by various ways and methods of solving

Other guidelines for selecting worthwhile problems are listed in Chapter 2. The last of these is the one we believe to be most important: that the *teacher* fully understand the mathematics in the problem, so that he or she can better facilitate student understanding. The real test of quality for a problem is whether it works for students and engages them in the process.

Many Websites for problem solving are available on the Internet, and educational publishers produce problem-solving components in their math text series. An effective way to create a grade-level collection of problems is to have all teachers in a grade level try problems in their own classrooms and share those problems with one another. In this way, each teacher will begin compiling a folder of problems that have been tried in the classroom and that match grade-level standards and particular topics of conceptual units.

Q. *How do I give a grade based on the problem-solving rubric?*

A. The main purpose of a problem-solving rubric is to provide feedback to students on their problem-solving ability, so that they have the opportunity to note where they are doing well and where they need to improve. A rubric should be designed to provide criteria for an overall performance level, not a percentage or point value. When giving a grade for problem solving within a traditional grading system, be careful that the point value, percentage score, or letter grade given reflects what is most important in students' performance: their understanding of the *mathematics*, not the criteria that have nothing to do with the actual mathematics (i.e., following directions, effort, language conventions, and so on).

Q. *Which type of rubric works best for the problem-solving activity?*

A. Either a holistic or an analytic rubric works fine for problem solving. An analytic rubric provides teachers and students with specific feedback relative to each major component within the rubric (e.g., mathematical process, strategies, vocabulary, and so on). The drawback of using an analytic rubric is that it may be too complicated to use or confusing to students. When using an analytic rubric in a traditional grading system, the letter grade or percentage derived from it can be very misleading in terms of determining student understanding of the mathematics in the problem. If a point system is attached to the criteria in an analytic rubric, students can gather points for items that do not relate to the mathematics and thus misleadingly inflate the student's overall performance.

We recommend using a holistic rubric designed for use with every Problem-Solving Task, such as the one presented in Chapter 2. Not only is it easier to use, but it also keeps both students and teachers sharply focused on the evidence of student understanding and on the mathematics used to solve the problem.

Step 3: Conceptual Understanding

Q. *I'm used to using a textbook for math instruction. How can I adjust to the conceptual unit approach?*

A. A textbook should be a resource to help you teach the standards at your grade level. If you are used to following a textbook as your guide for instruction, an easy way to transition to a conceptual unit approach is to start by examining your grade-level standards and identifying which standards are presented effectively by the textbook and which are not. For standards that are not effectively presented in the textbook, collaborate with other grade-level teachers and design a unit of study using the guidelines presented in Chapter 3. Another suggestion is to design just one conceptual unit per quarter when first implementing the *Five Easy Steps* program; then build to two per quarter the next year; and so on.

Q. *How many Conceptual Understanding Units should I teach each year?*

A. The number of units you develop and teach depends on your particular grade level and how effectively your math standards can be grouped around a common topic. All math is interrelated, but for the sake of instruction you want to be able to determine four or five essential mathematical understandings for one unit of study. Typically, teachers using the *Five Easy Steps* program develop approximately six conceptual units of instruction during the course of a school year.

Q. *How can I teach Conceptual Understanding Units of instruction and still cover all the standards for my grade level? There is not enough time to have students fully understand what they are doing. I have to keep moving, or I will fall behind the pace established by my district. Why should I consider this approach?*

A. The conceptual unit approach to teaching mathematics is based on teaching for understanding, not on covering material. There is no educational support for the idea that just covering learning objectives helps students learn that information. Therefore, the choice each of us has to make is this: Do I help my students *understand* mathematics, or do I move on whether they know

Typically, teachers using the Five Easy Steps *program develop approximately six conceptual units of instruction during the course of a school year.*

it or not? Learning mathematics is a building process. If a strong foundation of understanding is not established, teachers can cover, cover, cover all they want, and students will just get further and further behind. That is why we strongly endorse the practice of identifying math Power Standards—those *prioritized* standards that all students need for success each year in school, in life, and on all high-stakes assessments.

Q. *How does the conceptual unit approach help test scores?*

A. Helping students deeply understand essential concepts and skills they are expected to know and be able to do will always help test scores. The conceptual unit approach is intentionally designed to develop student understanding around essential grade-level math standards (Power Standards). Following the process outlined in Chapter 3 will help teachers design and teach conceptual units matched to grade-level math expectations. This is a powerful practice that is sure to prepare students for success, not only on state assessments, but also in understanding and applying math in succeeding years of school and throughout their lives.

Q. *Why should students understand mathematics conceptually? I learned math procedurally, and I did fine. I made it through college by memorizing procedures.*

A. Learning math procedurally means memorizing a series of steps to get an answer. Procedural mathematics is very answer-focused, and not at all meaning-based. Conceptual instruction allows students to make sense of mathematics, to see the patterns and connections within mathematics, while learning a concept and then the procedure attached to that concept.

A series of memorized steps is easily forgotten and easily mixed up with other memorized steps.

Math textbooks in this country have become longer and longer because each year students have to review what they supposedly learned in the preceding grade. Furthermore, teaching mathematics without attached meaning has become an issue of equity in the United States. Many students are not successful in math because math never made sense to them. It has even become acceptable in our culture to say, "I'm not a math person." Continuing this type of instructional approach and mindset prevents many students from achieving their full potential as mathematically powerful students.

Q. *How long should a Conceptual Understanding Unit last?*

A. A conceptual unit will usually last a few weeks, as described in Chapter 3. However, the actual length of your unit will depend on the amount of time you dedicate to actual math instruction on a daily basis. The number of standards related to a particular topic usually determines the duration of the unit.

Q. *I noticed in the recommended schedule for my specific grade level that you assign homework, but no time was allocated for the processing of that homework the next day. When do you go over homework?*

A. Assigned homework should relate to the instruction that students are receiving within the conceptual unit. Effective homework gives students the opportunity to practice the skills or concepts that they are learning in school. Such homework can be quickly reviewed at the beginning of the conceptual unit instruction portion of the math period.

Q. *My district has a pacing chart for instruction in math, and we are all expected to follow it. How does the conceptual unit approach fit with this situation?*

A. Pacing charts can make teaching for understanding a real challenge. Douglas B. Reeves, nationally recognized expert on standards, assessment, and accountability, often says this in his keynote addresses regarding the use of pacing charts:

> There is not a single state standard that requires students to "do algebra quickly." Rather, the standards require them to do algebra, and every other subject, proficiently. This emphasis on proficiency explicitly rejects speed as a criterion for evaluation, unless (as in keyboarding, for example) speed is inherent in proficiency. In the vast majority of performances in school as well as the world of work, the most effective model is not one of hasty, slipshod work. It is a process of submitting work, getting feedback on the work, and improving the work. This is what great leaders and teachers do in all subjects and in all walks of life.

The reasoning that all students will learn a math concept by a certain date is a bit dumbfounding. However, if teachers follow the process outlined in Chapter 3, they can still effectively use standards to determine what is essential to teach for student understanding. It all comes down to maintaining a sharp focus on what is truly critical for students to know and be able to do mathematically. Using each of the five steps of this model will help all students become successful in mathematics, even within the constraints of a district pacing chart. Teachers should trust their professional judgment and modify or adjust any preset instructional pace so as to meet the learning needs of their students. They must also consider the negative effects on student learning and retention if they do not.

Q. *How can I teach for understanding if I don't understand the mathematics myself?*

A. The steps outlined in this book are designed primarily to help your students become successful at mathematics, but they are also designed to help the classroom teacher feel more confident about teaching for understanding. Learning any new professional practice can be a bit uncomfortable, but allow yourself time to follow the guidelines in the book. You will find that your attitude toward and confidence with math will improve. You will find that you can indeed understand mathematics, and that you can do a more effective job of teaching it than you might have thought!

Q. *I know that other countries teach math differently than we do in the United States and get very good results. How do other countries develop units of study in mathematics?*

A. Asian countries, for example, use a method called "Lesson Study" to develop their curricula in mathematics. The process is highly collaborative. Teachers design lessons together, watch each other teach those lessons, and then revise the lessons based on professional feedback. Asian teachers also use the knowledge package idea (described in Chapter 3) to determine all the components of math that connect to the concept they will be teaching in a conceptual unit of instruction. This results in effective lessons that are grouped into units of study and shared with all who teach that grade level.

Step 4: Mastery of Math Facts

Q: *We do a "Mad Minute" worksheet every day to start the math period. Won't that help my students memorize their facts?*

A. Timing students on their math facts does not teach them anything except to be nervous! The "Mad Minute" approach does not allow students to develop effective strategies for fact retrieval. It does not assist development of pattern knowledge, nor does it provide them with any information about the number system. Timing is part of assessment, not instruction. For further guidelines and information on this important question, please refer to Chapter 4.

Q. *Why do so many students not remember their math facts? I learned math facts from the drill-and-kill method. Why doesn't that work for my students?*

A. Actually, you most likely did not learn your facts from the drill-and-kill method; you remembered the facts because you were able to find a pattern or an association that allowed you to recall the facts when necessary. Students today do not remember math facts because of *the way* they are taught those facts. Most likely, they are not being intentionally led to discover the underlying concepts for learning math facts, which become evident when teachers emphasize the particular math-facts patterns appropriate for each grade level; rather, they are just expected to memorize the facts. Drill is effective only when it is drill of efficient strategies that the student has developed for fact retrieval. Math-fact retrieval is highly dependent on the development of strong number sense. Please refer to Chapter 1, in the sections related to Math Review, for ideas that will help students develop strong number sense, and also consult Chapter 4 for math-fact strategies.

Q. *Don't students have to prove that they know their math facts within a time constraint? Also, if I don't time my students, won't that affect their standardized test scores?*

A. One of the most frequent and problematic questions we hear from math teachers concerns students learning their math facts within timed-testing conditions. Educators ask, "To develop automaticity with regard to their math facts, don't students have to be timed? Isn't speed essential?"

Automatic retrieval of math facts comes when students develop effective strategies for retrieval based on their knowledge of the number system. Practice with strategies that are effective and reliable for each student is the key to automatic retrieval. Mental Math activities are excellent for helping students develop strong number sense. Timing has nothing to do with students becoming proficient with math facts. Unfortunately, timing has led many students to decide that they are "bad at math." Timed math-fact recall must not continue to be the central issue: student *understanding* and *effective practice* of math facts are what we must emphasize.

Q. *What about students who count on their fingers to get the answer to a basic math fact?*

A. Students who are still counting on their fingers after first or second grade are letting the teacher know that they have not developed the idea of quantity, and that they have very limited number sense. The issue is not the use of their fingers, but that these students are *counting every thing individually, as opposed to considering patterns* within the number system. The information in this book about Math Review, Mental Math, and math facts offers effective ways to help students who still need to develop their number sense.

> *Automatic retrieval of math facts comes when students develop effective strategies for retrieval based on their knowledge of the number system.*

Q. *Should math-fact development be separate from the regular math program?*

A. Math-fact development should be *embedded* in daily math instruction. The Math Review and Mental Math processes will help you incorporate math-fact development within the regular math program.

Q. *How can parents play a part in their children's math-fact development?*

A. Parents can help their children develop number sense outside of school. Parents can ask their children to count by a given number, find combinations that make 5 and 10, talk about numbers, point out numbers when shopping or traveling, read books about numbers, and develop a positive attitude toward mathematics. They can play card and board games involving numbers with their children. Parents can engage children in measurement tasks at home and practice computing math problems mentally while driving to practices or appointments.

Closing Thoughts

We fully recognize the amount of initial thinking and preparation needed to implement a balanced math program, *because we have done this work ourselves.* Designing a conceptual unit for the first time may be challenging. The first time you present a Problem-Solving Task to your students may seem daunting. The first time you write a math rubric with colleagues or with your students may be as much of an education for you as it is for them. Once you have made each of these practices your own, though, you will be able to continuously refine that practice in the following months and years. When you can provide your students with the ingredients necessary to become mathematically powerful, we think you will agree that it was more than worth the effort.

If you have any questions that were not addressed in this or the previous chapters, or others that arise as you begin using these steps in your own classrooms, please do not hesitate to contact us. Our telephone numbers and e-mail addresses are in the "About the Authors" section at the beginning of the book. We will be more than happy to assist you in any way we can.

Best wishes as you begin balancing your math program in *Five Easy Steps*!

Guidelines for School Leaders

CHAPTER 10

As instructional leaders, school administrators often request guidelines for overseeing the effective implementation of the Five Easy Steps *math program in their individual schools. In this final chapter, we provide several documents that school leaders can use for this purpose.*

Executive Summary

This first document is an executive summary of the balanced math program. It provides an overview and a brief description of each of the steps. Administrators may duplicate this document to share and discuss with central office administrators, parents, and faculty.

Five Easy Steps to a Balanced Math Program
An Overview for Leaders and Leadership Teams
By Larry Ainsworth and Jan Christinson

Each step in the *Five Easy Steps to a Balanced Math Program* focuses on a different but interdependent practice that will help all students in grades K–12 become, in time, mathematically powerful. To realize the best results, the authors recommend that teachers follow the guidelines for effective implementation presented in the three books (primary, upper elementary, and secondary editions) and in the handout received at the *Five Easy Steps* workshop. Also, note that there is a suggested time frame in each of these resources that teachers can follow to make the steps manageable during a math lesson that takes approximately one hour.

Step 1: Computational Skills (Math Review and Mental Math). Math Review and Mental Math are daily practices designed to keep students "skill sharp" with regard to math concepts and procedures they have learned in prior lessons and units of study. Math Review is especially valuable in helping students: (1) remember what they were taught days, weeks, or months earlier; (2) apply or extend that learning as they encounter new concepts and skills; and (3) carry forward what they have learned into succeeding years. Math Review also helps close the gaps for students who are performing below proficiency on grade-level math standards, by providing daily practice and review of essential concepts and skills.

Math Review and Mental Math should be conducted *daily,* as described in the resources. The power of Math Review and Mental Math lies in regular practice. Teachers should *process* selected problems with students each day, emphasizing reasonable answers and the development of effective math strategies. Math Review and Mental Math can also provide teachers with a daily opportunity to introduce and maintain key math vocabulary. An accountability quiz (the Math Review Quiz) should be given every week, or every other week at the least, to inform teacher instruction and pinpoint needed interventions or accelerations for students. Students are encouraged to self-assess their own progress, identify where they need to improve, and develop a plan to achieve that improvement.

Step 2: Problem Solving. The Problem-Solving Task Write-Up Guide templates—different ones are provided in the texts for primary, upper elementary, and secondary grades—provide a simple but effective framework within which students learn to solve multiple-step math problems. First, students use calculation and graphic representation (words, pictures, and/or numbers) to solve the given problem, and then write a description, in their own words, of the process they followed. It is recommended that students practice the problem-solving write-up process on a regular basis throughout the school year until they are able to complete it independently. Teachers should select engaging, multiple-step problems that relate to the conceptual math units being taught (particularly those aligned to the math Power Standards) so that students can *apply* the mathematics they are learning to real-life math contexts. A generic problem-solving rubric is developed by individual grade levels or grade spans (primary, upper elementary, secondary) to assess student work. As with the Math Review (accountability) Quiz, students are encouraged to self-assess their own progress, identify where they need to improve, and develop a plan to achieve that improvement.

Step 3: Conceptual Understanding. To deepen students' conceptual understanding, it is essential that teachers deliver conceptual units of instruction based on key "unwrapped" math Power Standards aligned to end-of-unit assessment tasks. It is recommended that teachers design and teach a Conceptual Understanding Unit concerning math concepts and skills that are the most difficult for students to grasp. The recommended sequence for designing conceptual units is presented in each of the *Five Easy Steps* books. Participating teachers design a Conceptual Understanding Unit during the *Five Easy Steps* workshop. Schools are encouraged to create a "bank" of math conceptual units, with performance-based assessments, to help busy teachers work smarter, not harder.

Step 4: Mastery of Math Facts. Math-fact mastery is the responsibility of elementary schools. Students should enter middle school with their math facts learned. To achieve a systematic plan to ensure this, teachers within each elementary school—working with their administrators—first collaboratively determine which math facts are appropriate for student mastery *by the end of* each school year. They cross-reference their selections with the state standards and make whatever modifications are necessary to their grade-level assignment of facts. They then create a "math-facts map" that identifies which facts are to be mastered at each grade level, beginning with kindergarten and ending with grade 5. Lastly, a math-facts assessment schedule is developed for each grade. The grade-assigned facts and assessment schedule are then published and explained to both students and parents. A key emphasis in the *Five Easy Steps* approach to mastery of math facts is that students first learn the facts through an emphasis on discovering mathematical patterns, rather than rote drill or memorization.

Step 5: Common Formative Assessment. This final step is a grade-level math assessment *for* learning that participating teachers collaboratively design, administer, score, and analyze in order to differentiate instruction. These common formative assessments should be designed to assess *only* the math Power Standards. They are aligned to conceptual end-of-unit assessments in the classroom. Common formative assessments are typically based on a pre-/post-assessment design model and administered multiple times during the school year. Assessment items should represent different formats, including selected response, short constructed-response, and extended response. Teachers often choose to make these formats similar to those used on state assessments. This multiple-measures approach to assessment typically provides broader insights into student understanding. The teachers analyze the results of the student assessments in order to set a short-term instructional goal, and then select effective teaching strategies to achieve it. The student assessment results are used to

Executive Summary

inform and differentiate instruction so that the diverse learning needs of all students are met. When aligned to district quarterly math assessments, end-of-course math assessments, and even state math assessments, common formative assessments provide predictive value as to how students are likely to do on those external assessments—in time for teachers to make needed modifications in instruction.

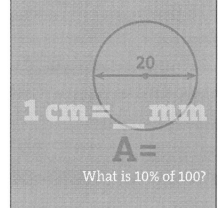

Math Leadership Team Planning Questions

Rather than assign the full responsibility for the implementation of *Five Easy Steps* to the principal or assistant principal alone, more and more schools are assembling school leadership teams comprised of the school administrator *and* grade-level or department representatives. It is their collective responsibility to oversee the effective implementation of *Five Easy Steps* in their building. This second document lists specific questions related to each of the steps to assist the school leadership team with planning.

Five Easy Steps to a Balanced Math Program
Math Leadership Team Planning Questions
By Jan Christinson and Larry Ainsworth

Step 1: Computational Skills (Math Review and Mental Math)

- Is every classroom implementing Math Review and Mental Math?

- How consistently are both of these practices being used in each grade level or department?

- Do teachers emphasize reasonable answer and math strategies with students when they process daily Math Review problems?

- What kinds of Math Review formats are teachers using at each grade level?

- What core math vocabulary should teachers introduce and maintain at each grade level?

- Are teachers emphasizing math vocabulary in Math Review and Mental Math?

- How often are teachers administering the Math Review (accountability) Quiz?

- Who provides the problems, individual teachers or grade-level teams?

- What additional resources or training do teachers need?

- Do new teachers know how to use Math Review and Mental Math?

Step 2: Problem Solving

- What should problem solving look like at each grade level and in each course?

- Which core problem-solving strategies should all teachers be using?

- Are students learning these same core problem-solving strategies?

- Are grade-level teams selecting or creating multiple-step problems that match the Conceptual Understanding Units being taught?

- How often are grade levels administering the Problem-Solving Task Write-Up work?

- How are teachers assessing problem solving? (individual teacher rubric, grade-level rubric, grade-span rubric, district-wide rubric)

- Are students involved in self- and peer-assessment?

- Are students reflecting on their progress (where they are doing well, where they need to improve)? Are we helping students to develop improvement goals?

- What training or support do teachers need to incorporate problem solving on a regular basis?

Step 3: Conceptual Understanding

- How is the school leadership team encouraging conceptual teaching (teaching for meaning) in mathematics?

- How can we help all teachers do more conceptual teaching?

- Which of our teachers could mentor other teachers in this regard?

- Which prioritized math standards (Power Standards) should all teachers be emphasizing at each grade?

- Are teachers "unwrapping" the math Power Standards for their grades? Is this happening in each classroom?

- Are teachers determining Big Ideas and Essential Questions to guide and focus their instruction and assessments?

- What grade-level Conceptual Understanding Units are teachers designing for topics that are particularly challenging for students to learn?

- Are the conceptual units aligned with end-of-unit assessments and accompanying rubrics or scoring guides?

- Are we creating a bank of grade-level conceptual units that all teachers can contribute to and use?

Step 4: Mastery of Math Facts

- Does the school have a plan that vertically maps the math facts in all four basic operations across the K–5 grades? Does this plan reflect or clarify the math facts listed in the state standards?

Math Leadership Team Planning Questions

- Is a math-facts assessment schedule in place at each grade?
- Do parents and students understand the school-wide math-facts plan and grade-specific assessment schedule?
- What help do teachers need to teach math facts through patterns, as opposed to drill and rote memorization only?
- What resources do teachers need to teach and assess their students' grasp of grade-level math facts?

Step 5: Common Formative Math Assessments

- Which grades are administering common math assessments *for* learning? How often?
- Are these assessments aligned to the math Power Standards?
- Are these assessments aligned to the district quarterly math assessments?
- Are grade levels collaboratively designing and scoring these assessments?
- Do these assessments include more than one format (selected response, short-constructed response, extended response)?
- Are grade levels analyzing the student data in grade-level or department Data Teams?
- Are assessment results being used to differentiate instruction (intervening for students at risk and accelerating for proficient and advanced students)?

6. Time Line

- Which of the *Five Easy Steps* will be our priority for school-wide implementation this year? Next year? The year after that?
- What is our projected date for complete school-wide implementation of all five steps?
- Have we prioritized our action plans to accomplish the most important tasks first?

Alignment Diagram

Educators and leaders are rightfully demanding to know how any new initiative or practice fits into the larger picture of standards, assessment, and accountability. The following diagram (introduced and explained in Chapter 5) represents the integration and interdependency of these practices. For a detailed description of this diagram and how each practice is closely and deliberately aligned with the others, please refer to *Common Formative Assessments: How to Connect Standards-Based Instruction and Assessment* (Ainsworth & Viegut, 2006). This diagram represents the interface of these practices with the *Five Easy Steps to a Balanced Math Program*.

Alignment Diagram

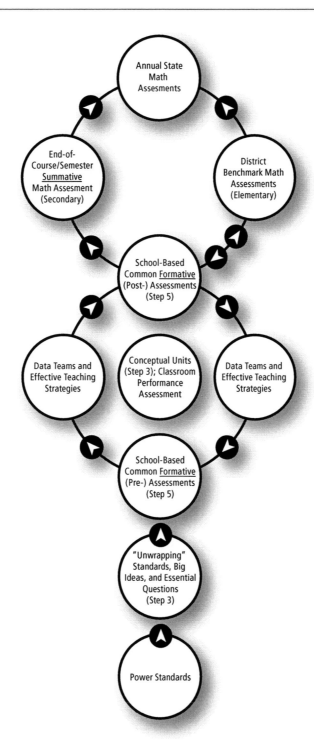

Adapted from *Common Formative Assessments: How to Connect Standards-Based Instruction and Assessment* (Ainsworth & Viegut, Corwin Press, 2006).

A Framework for Implementation

This final document provides a three-column template that school leaders or school leadership teams can use as a planning blueprint for effective implementation of each of the *Five Easy Steps*. The authors would like to acknowledge and thank Laura Besser of the Center for Performance Assessment for developing this template, into which we inserted the content relevant to *Five Easy Steps*.

The descriptions in the "Desired State" column represent key indicators of full implementation that leaders should expect to see when the steps are fully implemented in individual classrooms and grade levels. Readers are encouraged to add other indicators of their choice.

To use this planning blueprint effectively, we recommend that the school leadership team conduct an honest assessment of the school's current reality with regard to each of the five steps. The team can then record those indicators in the "Current State" column.

When the first column is completed, record in the middle column the "Action Steps" that your leadership team and faculty members will need to take to achieve the indicators in the "Desired State" column. As part of this last step, it may be necessary first to identify the obstacles (perceived or real) standing in the way of effective implementation of each action step. During the process of identifying those obstacles, the needed action steps may become readily apparent.

Once this is finished, draft a preliminary time frame for the first year of implementation. When ready, repeat the process for the second and third years of implementation. These timelines should remain flexible and be adjusted as the school moves through the process. However, adhering to a short- and long-term schedule, as much as possible, will help the school stay on track toward achieving the "Desired State" goals.

Two blank, full-size versions of the planning template appear in the "Reproducibles" section at the end of this book.

It is our hope that these documents, individually and collectively, will assist leaders and leadership teams in implementing and sustaining *Five Easy Steps to a Balanced Math Program*. Again, please contact the authors at the phone numbers or e-mail addresses provided in the "About the Authors" section at the beginning of this book should you have further questions.

A Framework for Implementing
Five Easy Steps to a Balanced Math Program

What do math instruction and assessment *currently* look like in our school? (Sample responses)

Math Instruction	Math Assessment
• Varied approaches and styles • Mainly traditional approach • Textbook-driven • More lecture, less student involvement • Teacher-centered • Learning targets not always clear • Chapter-based vs. standards-based • Inch-deep, mile-wide coverage • Differentiation, but not enough to meet wide diversity of student needs • Monitoring/adjustment of instruction • Practice worksheets • Some peer tutoring • Some cooperative learning	• More summative than formative • Chapter and unit tests • District benchmark "dipstick" quarterly math assessments aligned to the state test • End-of-course assessments at secondary level • Certain schools are beginning to use common math assessments • Assessment not used to drive instruction

A Framework for Implementation

Key for *Five Easy Steps* Terms

CFA	Common Formative Assessment	**MR**	Math Review
FES	Five Easy Steps	**PS**	Power Standards
MM	Mental Math	**PST**	Problem-Solving Task

STEP 1: Computational Skills (Math Review and Mental Math)

Current State	Action Steps	Desired State
<ul><li></li><li></li><li></li><li></li><li></li><li></li><li></li><li></li></ul>	<ul><li></li><li></li><li></li><li></li><li></li><li></li><li></li><li></li></ul>	<ul><li>All grades using MR and MM daily</li><li>Teacher-designed problems based on current needs of students</li><li>Teachers emphasize reasonable answer and math strategies with students during processing of MR problems</li><li>Math Review Quiz given weekly or biweekly</li><li>Appropriate MR formats used at each grade level</li><li>Math vocabulary incorporated into MR and MM</li></ul>

STEP 2: Problem Solving

Current State	Action Steps	Desired State
•	•	• Core problem-solving strategies identified and used by all teachers
•	•	• Core problem-solving strategies taught to students
•	•	• Grade-level teams select or create multistep PSTs that match Conceptual Understanding Units
•	•	• Grade levels administer a PST at least twice a month
•	•	• Problem solving assessed with generic rubric applicable to all PSTs
•	•	• Students involved in self- and peer-assessment
•	•	• Students reflect on their progress (where they are doing well, where they need to improve) and develop goal/plan for improvement
•	•	• Ongoing support for teachers identified and provided as needed
•	•	

Step 3: Conceptual Understanding

Current State	Action Steps	Desired State
•	•	• Conceptual teaching taking place at every grade level
•	•	• Grade-level mentor teachers assist colleagues with conceptual teaching as needed
•	•	• Core math standards (PS) identified and emphasized in conceptual units of instruction
•	•	• Math standards "unwrapped" to pinpoint key concepts and skills
•	•	• Big Ideas and Essential Questions used to focus instruction and assessment
•	•	• Math vocabulary identified and emphasized at each grade level
•	•	• Grade-level conceptual units, including aligned end-of-unit assessments, used to teach students "unwrapped" math PS concepts and skills
•	•	• School and/or district bank of grade-level math conceptual units established, for all teachers to use and contribute to

Step 4: Mastery of Math Facts

Current State	Action Steps	Desired State
•	•	• School plan in place that vertically maps all math facts in the four basic operations across grades K–5
•	•	• School plan reflects or clarifies the math facts listed in state standards
•	•	• Math-facts assessment schedule in place at each grade
•	•	• Parents and students understand school-wide plan and grade-specific assessment schedule
•	•	• Math facts taught through patterns, rather than memorization only
•	•	• Necessary resources are available for teaching and assessing students' mastery of grade-level math facts
•	•	
•	•	
•	•	

A Framework for Implementation

Step 5: Common Formative Assessment

Current State	Action Steps	Desired State
•	•	• Grade levels administer collaboratively designed, short-cycle math assessments *for* learning
•	•	• CFAs aligned to math PS and classroom end-of-unit assessments
•	•	• Assessments aligned to district quarterly math assessments
•	•	• CFAs include more than one type of format (selected response, short-constructed response, extended response)
•	•	• Grade levels collaboratively score math CFAs
•	•	• Grade levels analyze student data in grade-level or department Data Teams
•	•	• Assessment results used to differentiate instruction (interventions for students at risk and accelerations for proficient and advanced students)
•	•	
•	•	

Five Easy Steps Prioritized Time Frame for Implementation

Time Frame—Year 1	What We Want to Have in Place
September 2006	•
October 2006	•
November 2006	•
December 2006	•
January 2007	•
February 2007	•
March 2007	•
April 2007	•
May 2007	•
June 2007	•
Summer 2007	•

A Framework for Implementation

Five Easy Steps **Prioritized Time Frame for Implementation** (Continued)

Time Frame—Year 2	What We Want to Have in Place
August 2007	•
September 2007	•
October 2007	•
November 2007	•
December 2007	•
January 2008	•
February 2008	•
March 2008	•
April 2008	•
May 2008	•
Summer 2008	•

(continues)

Five Easy Steps Prioritized Time Frame for Implementation *(Continued)*

Time Frame—Year 3	What We Want to Have in Place
August 2008	•
September 2008	•
October 2008	•
November 2008	•
December 2008	•
January 2009	•
February 2009	•
March 2009	•
April 2009	•
May 2009	•
Summer 2009	•

Reproducibles

In this section we have included reproducible versions of templates and charts that appear within the chapters. The reader has permission to duplicate these for instructional use only.

They are presented in the following sequence:

Step 1: Computational Skills (Math Review and Mental Math). There are three templates that can be used for a given week of Math Review and Mental Math. The third template is for the teacher to copy and use as an overhead each day.

Step 2: Problem Solving. We have provided two sample Problem-Solving Task Write-Up Guides and a recommended problem-solving rubric. The first write-up guide is designed for upper elementary grades, but may be appropriate for use by secondary grades when the process is first introduced to students. The second write-up guide is designed for middle school and high school students. Also included is a summary of problem-solving steps written specifically for students in secondary grades. In addition, we have included a summary of steps for the alternative problem-solving method with an accompanying write-up guide.

Step 3: Conceptual Understanding. Included here is the template used to design a conceptual unit, with all the components described in Chapter 3 and illustrated with grade-specific examples in Chapters 6, 7, and 8.

Step 4: Mastery of Math Facts. Because mastery of math facts is an instructional responsibility assigned to elementary-grade teachers, we have not included any examples here. However, a summary of patterns by grade, and suggestions for daily practice, are included here to guide teachers in assisting students who are still struggling to master their math facts.

Step 5: Common Formative Assessment. The *Five Easy Steps* Balanced Math Alignment Diagram that appears in Chapter 5 is reproduced here as a "big picture" that shows the interrelationships between the *Five Easy Steps* framework and other powerful practices related to standards, assessment, and accountability. We have also included, at the end of this section, two copies of the template that appears in Chapter 10, "A Framework for Implementing *Five Easy Steps to a Balanced Math Program*." Educators and leaders can use this template to plan for the successful implementation of each of the five steps over three successive years.

Daily Math Review

Name _____

Monday

Place Value   Fraction Operations   Decimals

Exponents   Geometry   Bonus

Mental Math   **1.** _____   **2.** _____   **3.** _____

Tuesday

Place Value   Fraction Operations   Decimals

Exponents   Geometry   Bonus

Mental Math   **1.** _____   **2.** _____   **3.** _____

Daily Math Review

Name _____

Wednesday

Place Value	Fraction Operations	Decimals

Exponents	Geometry	Bonus

Mental Math   1. _____   2. _____   3. _____

Thursday

Place Value	Fraction Operations	Decimals

Exponents	Geometry	Bonus

Mental Math   1. _____   2. _____   3. _____

Five Easy Steps to a Balanced Math Program for Secondary Grades

Daily Math Review Overhead

Name _____

Place Value	**Fraction Operations**	**Decimals**

Exponents	**Geometry**	**Bonus**

Mental Math

1. _____   2. _____   3. _____

Problem-Solving Task Write-Up Guide: Middle School and High School

Data Sheet:

1. Head a piece of paper with your name, the date, the title of the problem (if given), and the words "Data Sheet."

2. Show *all* the work you did to solve the problem, using computation and/or graphic representation (words, pictures, and/or numbers).

3. Number each step as you work to solve the problem.

4. Write a number sentence that matches the problem.

5. Write a word sentence at the end of your Data Sheet that states the answer to the problem.

Write-Up:

Head a separate piece of paper:

1. Write your name, the date, and the title of the problem (if given), and the words "Write-Up" at the top of this paper.

2. Copy the title of each paragraph before you write your sentences for that paragraph.

3. Use the space below to complete your write-up. Everything you write must refer to the **math content, procedures you followed,** and **strategies you used** to solve the problem.

Paragraph One: Problem Statement

This problem is called _____ . It is about _____ .

I'm supposed to find _____ .

Paragraph Two: Work Write-Up

(It is understood that you have first read the problem and circled or underlined the key words. Do not include these steps in your write-up.) Explain **step by step,** in detail, everything you did **mathematically** to complete your Data Sheet and arrive at your answer. Refer back to your numbered steps on the Data Sheet to help you. Write this as if you were writing a recipe for someone to follow or giving a friend exact directions to your house. Use as many of these transition words as you need to describe each of your math steps: *first, next, then, after that, finally.*

Paragraph Three: Answer

My answer is _____ . I think my answer makes sense because _____ . (Verify or prove your answer by referring to the *math* you did. It is not enough just to write that you checked it on the calculator, or that you checked it twice, or that a friend or parent or teacher told you so.)

Problem-Solving Task Write-Up Guide: Middle School and High School

1. Problem Statement:

Rewrite the problem in your own words so that someone reading your paper could understand exactly what you were asked to do. Be sure to include the question you want to answer.

2. Plan:

Tell what you will do to solve the problem. Which strategy or strategies will you use? Before you begin work, develop a reasonable answer to the problem.

3. Work:

Show *all* the work you did to solve the problem on your Data Sheet. Use a table, graph, picture, chart, and/or calculations. Explain in detail what you did so that the reader will understand your work and how you arrived at an answer.

4. Answer:

Write your answer to the problem in a sentence. Verify your answer using mathematics. Could there be any other answers? Compare your answer to the reasonable estimate you made in step 2. Write what you learned from this problem that could help you to solve other problems.

Source: Adapted from Arlette Byrne, Valley Middle School, Carlsbad Unified School District, Carlsbad, CA.

Name _____ Title of Problem _____

Problem-Solving Scoring Guide: Middle School and High School

Exemplary:

- ❏ All "Proficient" criteria *plus*:
- ❏ Verifies answer mathematically
- ❏ Written work explains verification of answer

Proficient:

- ❏ Correct answer
- ❏ Solves problem on Data Sheet using computation and/or graphic representation
- ❏ Written explanation matches Data Sheet
- ❏ Shows correct mathematical reasoning
- ❏ Uses math vocabulary appropriate to problem
- ❏ Follows all Problem-Solving Guide directions to complete write-up

Progressing:

- ❏ Meets 4–5 of the "Proficient" criteria

Beginning:

- ❏ Meets fewer than 4 of the "Proficient" criteria
- ❏ Task to be repeated after remediation

Peer's Evaluation _____

I think this score is a _____ because _____

Self-Evaluation _____

I think my score is a _____ because _____

Teacher's Evaluation _____ because _____

_____

Note: Proficiency must address the *mathematics.*

Students have ongoing opportunities to reflect upon and revise their work with feedback from the scoring guide.

Problem-Solving Guidelines for Secondary Students

Get Ready to Solve the Problem.

1. Read the problem first.
2. Underline or circle the important facts and key words.
3. What are you supposed to find out?
4. Are there any "tricky" parts to the problem?
5. What math vocabulary words are in the problem?
6. Which math strategies will you use?
7. What math tools might help you solve the problem?

Solve the Problem.

1. Solve the problem using calculation and graphic representation.
2. Number each of your problem-solving steps (1, 2, 3, . . .) on your Data Sheet.
3. Write a number sentence, equation, and/or formula to match the problem.
4. Write an explanation to match each of your steps on the Data Sheet.
5. Prove or verify your answer.

Write How You Solved the Problem.

1. Find the first math step you did on your Data Sheet (the step labeled #1).
2. Write one or two sentences that explain what you did.
3. Find the second math step you did on your Data Sheet (the step labeled #2).
4. Write one or two sentences that explain what you did.
5. Continue this way until you have written one or more sentences for each of the other numbered math steps, using transition words (*next, then, after that, finally*) as needed.
6. Include math vocabulary appropriate to the problem or task.
7. Check each sentence to make sure it describes a *math step.*
8. Check to make sure each sentence makes sense.

Want a Bonus Challenge?

1. Can you add the word *because* after each math step you write and then explain why you did that step?
2. Can you include other math vocabulary words to help explain how you solved the problem?
3. Can you solve the problem in more than one way?
4. Can you find someone who solved it differently than you did?
5. Can you change the problem to make it more challenging?
6. Can you solve your own challenging problem?
7. Can you find someone else who will try to solve your problem?

The Alternative Problem-Solving Method—A Summary of Steps

Preparation:

1. Select an appropriate problem.

2. Assign students to small cooperative groups of three.

3. Distribute the problem and an alternative write-up guide.

4. Have students count off (students number themselves one, two, or three within each group).

5. Have students create a Data Sheet.

6. Explain the "hint" process to students.

Solve the Problem:

7. Let students attempt to solve the problem independently (5 minutes).

8. Students record their independent work.

9. Begin initial group work (10–12 minutes).

10. Have students record the initial group work.

11. Do the first rotation (students numbered "1" rotate to new groups).

12. Begin work with the second group (10–12 minutes).

13. Have students record the second group's new information.

14. Do the second rotation (students numbered "2" rotate to new groups).

15. Begin work with the third group (10–12 minutes).

16. Have students record the third group's new information. (*Note:* The "hint" process introduced in #6 is ongoing during group work.)

17. Ask students to complete the "Answer and Verification" section.

18. Create the final product independently (homework).

19. Process the solution (next day in class).

20. Assess the completed student work (peer, self-, and teacher evaluations).

Source: Developed by Jan Christinson.

Five Easy Steps to a Balanced Math Program for Secondary Grades

Alternative Problem-Solving Task Write-Up Guide

Name _____ Title of Problem _____

Independent Work:

Cooperative Work:

Answer and Verification:

Five Easy Steps to a Balanced Math Program

Step 3

Conceptual Understanding Unit Design Template

Grade Level: _____

Conceptual Unit Focus: _____

Standards and Indicators Matched to Unit Focus: _____

_____

"Unwrapped" <u>Concepts</u>:

"Unwrapped" Skills:

Topics or Context: (Specific lessons, textbook pages, learning activities teachers will use during unit)

(continues)

Conceptual Understanding Unit Design Template *(Continued)*

Knowledge Package Cluster:

Big Ideas:

_____

_____

_____

_____

_____

Essential Questions:

_____

_____

_____

_____

End-of-Unit Assessment:

(continues)

Conceptual Understanding Unit Design Template *(Continued)*

Scoring Guide

Exemplary:

❑ **All "Proficient" criteria** *plus*:

❑ _____

❑ _____

❑ _____

Proficient:

❑ _____

❑ _____

❑ _____

❑ _____

Progressing:

❑ _____

❑ _____

❑ _____

❑ _____

Beginning:

❑ _____

❑ _____

Peer's Evaluation (Optional) _____

Self-Evaluation _____

Teacher's Evaluation _____

Comments _____

_____

Five Easy Steps to a Balanced Math Program for Secondary Grades

Conceptual Understanding Unit Design Template *(Continued)*

**Lessons and Activities Students Need to Understand
"Unwrapped" Concepts, Skills, and Big Ideas:**

_____

_____

_____

_____

_____

_____

_____

_____

_____

_____

_____

_____

_____

_____

_____

_____

(continues)

Conceptual Understanding Unit Design Template *(Continued)*

Teacher Reflections:

1. *What worked? What didn't?* _____

_____

_____

_____

_____

2. *What will I do differently next time?*

_____

_____

_____

_____

3. *What student work samples do I have?*

_____

_____

_____

_____

4. *What suggestions can I provide for other teachers who may use this assessment?*

_____

_____

_____

_____

Step 4: Mastery of Math Facts

Using Patterns: A K–5 Summary

Patterns that will help K–2 students learn math facts and develop improved number sense include:

- One more than and two more than a number (8 + 1, 8 + 2, and so on)
- Facts with zero (0 + 2, 0 + 3, and so on)
- Doubles (2 + 2, 5 + 5, 9 + 9, and so on)
- Facts that make five (3 + 2, 2 + 3, and so on)
- Facts that make ten (7 + 3, 2 + 8, and so on)
- Part-part-whole relationships (fact-family groups)
- Addition and subtraction as inverse operations

Patterns by Grade

A grade-specific summary of the patterns used to teach students math facts follows:

Kindergarten:

- The quantity of a number
- How to correctly say a number
- One more than a number
- Doubles
- Addition facts that make five
- Part-part-whole relationships (fact-family groups)
- Addition facts that make ten

First Grade:

- Part-part-whole relationships (fact-family groups): 0 + 5 = 5 and 5 + 0 = 5; 1 + 4 = 5 and 4 + 1 = 5; 2 + 3 = 5 and 3 + 2 = 5, and so on with other fact-family groups
- Anchors of 5 and 10 (five-frame and ten-frame)
- Counting by a given number (2s, 5s, 10s)
- Two more and two less than a number
- Addition and subtraction as inverse operations

Second Grade:

- Part-part-whole relationships in addition: 5 + 3 = 8; 3 + 5 = 8; 6 + 2 = 8; and 2 + 6 = 8; and so on
- "Think addition" for subtraction facts
- Addition and subtraction as inverse operations

Third Grade:

- Part-part-whole relationships (3 + 5 = 8; 2 + 6 = 8; 4 + 4 = 8; 8 − 5 = 3; 8 − 6 = 2; and so on) in both addition and subtraction
- Regular practice with various patterns within multiplication facts (2s, 3s, 5s, 9s, 10s, and so on)
- Regular opportunities to develop a strong foundation with multiplication facts
- Strategy of "think multiplication" for division facts
- Multiplication and division as inverse operations

(continues)

Fourth Grade:

- Repeated practice with patterns within multiplication facts, division facts, and the number system (powers of 10)
- Strategy of "think multiplication" for division facts
- Multiplication and division as inverse operations
- Extend strategies to multidigit problems in Mental Math activities

Fifth Grade:

- Emphasize various patterns found within multiplication facts (i.e., 2s, 3s, 5s, 9s, 10s)
- Strategy of "think multiplication" with division facts
- Multiplication and division as inverse operations
- Determine a reasonable answer
- Apply math-facts strategies to multidigit problems provided during Mental Math activities

Middle School:

- The expectation is that students should enter middle school already having mastered their math facts.
- Middle school students should continue development of their number sense by receiving regular practice with the number-sense patterns and math-fact patterns developed in Grades K–5.

Suggestions for Daily Practice (Multiplication and Division)

- Orally practice all the twos, threes, fours, and so on with a family member, classmate, or teacher aide—first by groupings of like facts or in sequence, then at random, and finally with all the facts mixed together.
- Using flash cards, practice all the twos, threes, fours, and so on with a family member, classmate, or teacher aide—by groupings of like facts or in sequence, then at random, and then all together.
- Notice product *patterns* for multiplication:
  - Look at product patterns for five (0, 5, 10, 15, 20, 25, 30, 35, 40, 45) where the ones digit alternates between zero and five.
  - Look at product patterns of three (3, 6, 9 where 3 + 6 = 9) and the remaining products (12, 15, 18, 21, 24, 27) where the sum of the two digits equals three, six, or nine.
  - Look at product patterns of nine (9, 18, 27, 36, 45, 54, 63, 72, 81, 90) where the sum of the two digits equals nine, the tens digits are sequenced in order from one to nine, and the ones digits are sequenced in reverse, from nine to zero.
- Count aloud the multiples of a given number.
- Learn the "Fact Families" in addition, subtraction, multiplication, and division.
- Write math facts each day in school and at home.
- Play math-facts games on the Internet and utilize computer software math-facts programs.
- Use practice worksheets.
- Read literature books that involve adding, subtracting, multiplying, and dividing in the story line.

Five Easy Steps Balanced Math Alignment Diagram

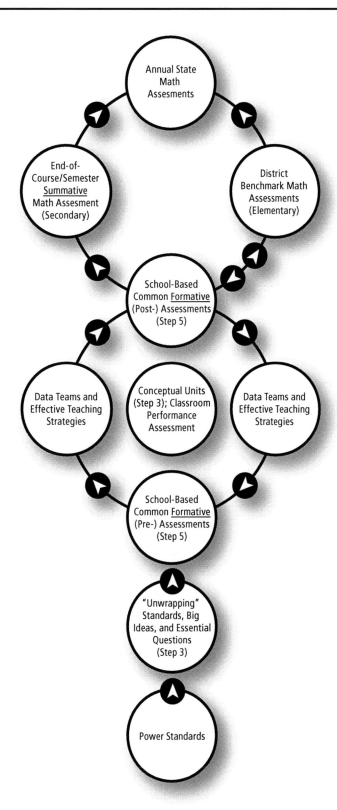

Adapted from *Common Formative Assessments: How to Connect Standards-Based Instruction and Assessment* (Ainsworth & Viegut, Corwin Press, 2006).

A Framework for Implementing

Five Easy Steps to a Balanced Math Program

What do math instruction and assessment *currently* look like in our school? (Sample responses)

Math Instruction	Math Assessment
• Varied approaches and styles • Mainly traditional approach • Textbook-driven • More lecture, less student involvement • Teacher-centered • Learning targets not always clear • Chapter-based vs. standards-based • Inch-deep, mile-wide coverage • Differentiation, but not enough to meet wide diversity of student needs • Monitoring/adjustment of instruction • Practice worksheets • Some peer tutoring • Some cooperative learning	• More summative than formative • Chapter and unit tests • District benchmark "dipstick" quarterly math assessments aligned to the state test • End-of-course assessments at secondary level • Certain schools are beginning to use common math assessments • Assessment not used to drive instruction

Key for *Five Easy Steps* Terms

CFA Common Formative Assessment   **MR** Math Review

FES Five Easy Steps   **PS** Power Standards

MM Mental Math   **PST** Problem-Solving Task

Step 1 Computational Skills (Math Review and Mental Math)

Current State	Action Steps	Desired State
•	•	• All grades using MR and MM daily
•	•	• Teacher-designed problems based on current needs of students
•	•	• Teachers emphasize reasonable answer and math strategies with students during processing of MR problems
•	•	• Math Review Quiz given weekly or biweekly
•	•	• Appropriate MR formats used at each grade level
•	•	• Math vocabulary incorporated into MR and MM
•	•	
•	•	
•	•	
•	•	

Step 2: Problem Solving

Current State	Action Steps	Desired State
•	•	• Core problem-solving strategies identified and used by all teachers
•	•	• Core problem-solving strategies taught to students
•	•	• Grade-level teams select or create multistep PSTs that match Conceptual Understanding Units
•	•	• Grade levels administer a PST at least twice a month
•	•	• Problem solving assessed with generic rubric applicable to all PSTs
•	•	• Students involved in self- and peer-assessment
•	•	• Students reflect on their progress (where they are doing well, where they need to improve) and develop goal/plan for improvement
•	•	• Ongoing support for teachers identified and provided as needed
•	•	
•	•	

Step 3: Conceptual Understanding

Current State	Action Steps	Desired State
•	•	• Conceptual teaching taking place at every grade level
•	•	• Grade-level mentor teachers assist colleagues with conceptual teaching as needed
•	•	• Core math standards (PS) identified and emphasized in conceptual units of instruction
•	•	• Math standards "unwrapped" to pinpoint key concepts and skills
•	•	• Big Ideas and Essential Questions used to focus instruction and assessment
•	•	• Math vocabulary identified and emphasized at each grade level
•	•	• Grade-level conceptual units, including aligned end-of-unit assessments, used to teach students "unwrapped" math PS concepts and skills
•	•	• School and/or district bank of grade-level math conceptual units established, for all teachers to use and contribute to
•	•	

Step 4: Mastery of Math Facts

Current State	Action Steps	Desired State
•	•	• School plan in place that vertically maps all math facts in the four basic operations across grades K–5
•	•	• School plan reflects or clarifies the math facts listed in state standards
•	•	• Math-facts assessment schedule in place at each grade
•	•	• Parents and students understand school-wide plan and grade-specific assessment schedule
•	•	• Math facts taught through patterns, rather than memorization only
•	•	• Necessary resources are available for teaching and assessing students' mastery of grade-level math facts
•	•	
•	•	
•	•	
•	•	
•	•	

Step 5: Common Formative Assessment

Current State	Action Steps	Desired State
•	•	• Grade levels administer collaboratively designed, short-cycle math assessments *for* learning
•	•	• CFAs aligned to math PS and classroom end-of-unit assessments
•	•	• Assessments aligned to district quarterly math assessments
•	•	• CFAs include more than one type of format (selected response, short-constructed response, extended response)
•	•	• Grade levels collaboratively score math CFAs
•	•	• Grade levels analyze student data in grade-level or department Data Teams
•	•	• Assessment results used to differentiate instruction (interventions for students at risk and accelerations for proficient and advanced students)
•	•	
•	•	
•	•	

Five Easy Steps Prioritized Time Frame for Implementation

Time Frame—Year 1	What We Want to Have in Place
September 2006	•
October 2006	•
November 2006	•
December 2006	•
January 2007	•
February 2007	•
March 2007	•
April 2007	•
May 2007	•
June 2007	•
Summer 2007	•

Five Easy Steps Prioritized Time Frame for Implementation

Time Frame—Year 2	What We Want to Have in Place
August 2007	•
September 2007	•
October 2007	•
November 2007	•
December 2007	•
January 2008	•
February 2008	•
March 2008	•
April 2008	•
May 2008	•
Summer 2008	•

Five Easy Steps Prioritized Time Frame for Implementation

Time Frame—Year 3	What We Want to Have in Place
August 2008	•
September 2008	•
October 2008	•
November 2008	•
December 2008	•
January 2009	•
February 2009	•
March 2009	•
April 2009	•
May 2009	•
Summer 2009	•

What do math instruction and assessment currently look like in our school? (Add bullets as needed.)

Math Instruction	Math Assessment
•	•
•	•
•	•
•	•
•	•
•	•
•	•
•	•
•	•
•	•
•	•
•	•

Step 1: Computational Skills (Math Review and Mental Math)

Current State	Action Steps	Desired State
•	•	•
•	•	•
•	•	•
•	•	•
•	•	•
•	•	•
•	•	•
•	•	•
•	•	•
•	•	•
•	•	•

Step 2: Problem Solving

Current State	Action Steps	Desired State
•	•	•
•	•	•
•	•	•
•	•	•
•	•	•
•	•	•
•	•	•
•	•	•
•	•	•
•	•	•
•	•	•

Step 3: Conceptual Understanding

Current State	Action Steps	Desired State
•	•	•
•	•	•
•	•	•
•	•	•
•	•	•
•	•	•
•	•	•
•	•	•
•	•	•
•	•	•
•	•	•
•	•	•

Five Easy Steps to a Balanced Math Program for Secondary Grades

Copyright © 2006 Center for Performance Assessment

Step 4: Mastery of Math Facts

Current State	Action Steps	Desired State
•	•	•
•	•	•
•	•	•
•	•	•
•	•	•
•	•	•
•	•	•
•	•	•
•	•	•
•	•	•
•	•	•

Step 5: Common Formative Assessment

Current State	Action Steps	Desired State
•	•	•
•	•	•
•	•	•
•	•	•
•	•	•
•	•	•
•	•	•
•	•	•
•	•	•
•	•	•
•	•	•

Five Easy Steps to a Balanced Math Program for Secondary Grades

Five Easy Steps Prioritized Time Frame for Implementation

Time Frame—Year 1	What We Want to Have in Place
August	•
September	•
October	•
November	•
December	•
January	•
February	•
March	•
April	•
May	•
Summer	•

Five Easy Steps Prioritized Time Frame for Implementation

Time Frame—Year 2	What We Want to Have in Place
August	•
September	•
October	•
November	•
December	•
January	•
February	•
March	•
April	•
May	•
Summer	•

Five Easy Steps Prioritized Time Frame for Implementation

Time Frame—Year 3	What We Want to Have in Place
August	•
September	•
October	•
November	•
December	•
January	•
February	•
March	•
April	•
May	•
Summer	•

References and Other Resources

References

Ainsworth, L. (2003a). *Power standards: Identifying the standards that matter the most.* Englewood, CO: Advanced Learning Press.

Ainsworth, L. (2003b). *"Unwrapping" the standards: A simple process to make standards manageable.* Englewood, CO: Advanced Learning Press.

Ainsworth, L., & Christinson, J. (2000). *Five easy steps to a balanced math program: A practical guide for K-8 classroom teachers.* Englewood, CO: Advanced Learning Press.

Ainsworth, L., & Christinson, J. (1998). *Student generated rubrics: An assessment model to help all students succeed.* New York: Dale Seymour Publications.

Ainsworth, L., & Viegut, D. (2006). *Common formative assessments: How to connect standards-based instruction and assessment.* Thousand Oaks, CA: Corwin Press.

Burns, M. (2004, October). Writing in math. *Education Leadership, 62*(2), 30–33.

Burns, M. (1999). Timed tests. In *Teaching children mathematics* (pp. 408–409). Sausalito, CA: NCTM.

Cawelti, G. (Ed.). (1999). *Handbook of research on improving student achievement* (2d ed.). Arlington, VA: Educational Research Service.

Christinson, J. (2005). *Nonfiction writing prompts for math for middle school.* (Write to Know series). Englewood, CO: Advanced Learning Press.

References and Other Resources

Guskey, T. R., & Bailey, J. M. (2001). *Developing grading and reporting systems for student learning.* Thousand Oaks, CA: Corwin Press.

Hiebert, J. (2003, April 2). Taped lessons offer insights into teaching. *Education Week, (22)*29, 1, 24.

Hiebert, J. (1997). *Making sense: Teaching and learning mathematics with understanding.* Portsmouth, NH: Heinemann Press.

Ma, L. (1999). *Knowing and teaching elementary mathematics.* Mahwah, NJ: Lawrence Erlbaum Associates.

Marzano, R. J. (2004). *Building background knowledge for academic achievement.* Alexandria, VA: ASCD.

Marzano, R. J. (2003). *What works in schools: Translating research into action.* Alexandria, VA: ASCD.

Marzano, R. J. (2001, September 15). How and why standards can improve student achievement: A conversation with Robert J. Marzano. *Educational Leadership, 59*(1), 14–15.

Marzano, R. J. (2000). *Transforming classroom grading.* Alexandria, VA: Association for Supervision and Curriculum Development.

National Council of Teachers of Mathematics. (2000). *Principles and standards for school mathematics.* Reston, VA: National Council of Teachers of Mathematics.

National Education Association. (2003). *Balanced assessment: The key to accountability and improved student learning.* Washington, DC: National Education Association.

O'Connor, K. (2002). *How to grade for learning: Linking grades to standards* (2d ed.). Glenview, IL: Pearson Education.

Reeves, D. B. (2004). The case against the zero. *Phi Delta Kappan, 86*(4), 324–325.

Seeley, C. L. (2005, December). Do the math in your head! *NCTM News Bulletin, (42)*5, 3.

References

Stiggins, R. J., Arter, J. A., Chappuis, J., & Chappuis, S. (2004). *Classroom assessment for student learning: Doing it right—using it well.* Portland, OR: Assessment Training Institute.

Van De Walle, J. (2004). *Elementary and middle school mathematics: Teaching developmentally* (5th ed.). Boston: Pearson.

Wiggins, G., & McTighe, J. (1998). *Understanding by design.* Alexandria, VA: ASCD.

Webliography of Online Math

A+ Math

    http://www.aplusmath.com/

AAA Math

    http://www.aaamath.com/

AIMS Puzzles

    http://www.aimsedu.org/Puzzle/PuzzleList.html

Algebra Help

    http://www.algebrahelp.com/index.jsp

Algebra links (Purplemath)

    http://www.purplemath.com/internet.htm

Algebra S.O.S. Math

    http://www.sosmath.com/algebra/algebra.html

Algebra Tutor

    http://www.algebratutor.org

All Math

    http://www.allmath.com/

Applets for Teachers

    http://www.geocities.com/appletsforteachers/

ArithmAttack

    http://www.dep.anl.gov/aattack.htm

Ask Dr. Math

    http://mathforum.org/dr.math/

Aunty Math/Math Challenges

    http://www.dupagechildrensmuseum.org/aunty/index.html

Calculators Online

    http://www.math.com/students/tools.html

Cats in Line Activity Page

    http://www.janbrett.com/piggybacks/ordinal.htm

Webliography of Online Math

Cool Math 4 Kids
   http://www.coolmath4kids.com/

Count On Math Games
   http://www.counton.org/

Count Us In Game
   http://www.abc.net.au/countusin/default.htm

Create a Graph
   http://nces.ed.gov/nceskids/Graphing/

Disaster Math Word Problems
   http://www.fema.gov/kids/dizmath.htm

Elementary Mathematics
   http://www.bcps.org/offices/lis/curric/elem/mathematics.html

Enchanted Mind Tangram Puzzle
   http://enchantedmind.com/puzzles/tangram/tangram.html

Fractals: Art or Math?
   http://www.dcet.k12.de.us/teach/quest/shari.htm

Franklin Institute Mathematics Hotlist
   http://www.fi.edu/tfi/hotlists/math.html

Fresh Baked Fractions
   http://www.funbrain.com/fract/index.html

Funbrain Math Games
   http://www.funbrain.com/

Gamequarium
   http://www.gamequarium.com/math.htm

Geometry Dictionary
   http://www.math.okstate.edu/~rpsc/dict/Dictionary.html

Geometry Online
   http://math.rice.edu/~lanius/Geom/

History of Mathematics Archive
   http://www-groups.dcs.st-and.ac.uk:80/~history/

iFigure: Online Calculators
    http://www.ifigure.com/

iMath Investigations
    http://illuminations.nctm.org/imath/

Improving Measurement & Geometry in Elementary Schools (IMAGES)
    http://www.dallassd.com/geometry/index.html

Interactive Mathematics
    http://www.cut-the-knot.org/content.shtml

Interactive Mathematics (Flash)
    http://teacherlink.org/content/math/interactive/flash/top.html

Interactive Word Problems
    http://www.geocities.com/Heartland/Ranch/2200/assess.htm

Kid's Clubhouse
    http://www.eduplace.com/kids/

Kids Domain Math Games
    http://www.kidsdomain.com/games/math2.html

King's Math Activities
    http://www.k111.k12.il.us/king/math.htm

Lemonade Stand
    http://www.lemonadegame.com/

Lite Brite (patterns)
    http://www.sfpg.com/animation/liteBrite.html

Magnetic Numbers
    http://home.freeuk.net/elloughton13/scramble1.htm

Math Cats
    http://www.mathcats.com/contents.html

Math Fact Cafe
    http://mathfactcafe.com/home/

Math Goodies
    http://www.mathgoodies.com/

Webliography of Online Math

Math in Daily Life
    http://www.learner.org/exhibits/dailymath/

Math Printables
    http://www.lr.k12.nj.us/ETTC/archives/drill.shtml

Math Stories (membership fee)
    http://www.mathstories.com

MathDrill
    http://www.mathdrill.com/index.php3

MathForum
    http://mathforum.org/

MATHGuide's Interactive Mathematics Lessons
    http://mathguide.com/lessons/

Mathnstuff.com
    http://www.mathnstuff.com

MathSURF Problem Solving
    http://www.mathsurf.com/teacher/index.html

Measure It!
    http://www.funbrain.com/measure/

Measure Your Weight on Other Worlds
    http://www.exploratorium.edu/ronh/weight/index.html

Measurement Games
    http://gamequarium.com/measurement.html

Measurement: Animal Weigh-In
    http://www.bbc.co.uk/education/mathsfile/shockwave/

MegaMathematics
    http://www.c3.lanl.gov/mega-math/

Megamaths
    http://www.bbc.co.uk/education/megamaths/tables.html

Moneyopolis
    http://www.moneyopolis.com/new/home.asp

Multiflyer

> http://www.gdbdp.com/multiflyer/

Multiplication Rock

> http://www.geocities.com/Athens/Academy/7303/M_Rock.html

National Library of Virtual Manipulatives

> http://matti.usu.edu/nlvm/nav/grade_g_2.html

National Math Trail

> http://www.nationalmathtrail.org/front2.html

Online Math Tools

> http://www.gamequarium.com/onlinemathtools.html

Pattern Blocks

> http://www.arcytech.org/java/patterns/patterns_j.shtml

PBS Mathline

> http://www.pbs.org/teachersource/math.htm?default

Peg Strategy Game

> http://scv.bu.edu/htbin/pegs

Ribbit's Math Ventures

> http://www.mohonasen.org/staffdev/mathven/Ribbit/rdefault.htm

Room 108 Math Activities

> http://www.netrover.com/~kingskid/108.html

Sea Shell Rounding Activity Page

> http://www.janbrett.com/piggybacks/rounding.htm

Snapdragon (Telling the Time)

> http://www.bbc.co.uk/wales/snapdragon/yesflash/intro.htm

Solving Math Word Problems

> http://studygs.net/mathproblems.htm

Stanley Park Chase (multiplication)

> http://www.bonus.com/bonus/card/stanley.bottom.html

Study Works: Puzzle of the Week (see also Puzzle Archives)

> http://www.studyworksonline.com/cda/justforfun/main/0,,NAV3-39,00.html

Suggested Reading

Take A Challenge
http://www.figurethis.org/index40.htm

Tangram Puzzle
http://www.fwend.com/tangram.htm

The Spanky Fractal Database
http://spanky.triumf.ca/

Visual Fractions
http://www.visualfractions.com

Word Problems for Kids
http://www.stfx.ca/special/mathproblems/welcome.html

Zone 101
http://www.zone101.com/Pages/zkids.htm

Suggested Reading

Center for Performance Assessment. (2005). *Nonfiction writing prompts for algebra.* (Write to Know series.) Englewood, CO: Advanced Learning Press.

Center for Performance Assessment. (2005). *Nonfiction writing prompts for geometry.* (Write to Know series.) Englewood, CO: Advanced Learning Press.

Chappuis, S., Stiggins, R. J., Arter, J., & Chappuis, J. (2004). *Assessment for learning: An action guide for school leaders.* Portland, OR: Assessment Training Institute.

Reeves, D. B. (2004). *Accountability for learning: How teachers and school leaders can take charge.* Alexandria, VA: Association for Supervision and Curriculum Development.

Index

Index

Index

collaboration on, 117, 124–27, 212, 217

design of, 148, 163, 177

end-of-unit assessment similarity to, 124, 148, 163, 177

item types, 125

for learning, 14, 18, 85, 212, 217, 227, 257

math-facts schedule, 212, 217, 226, 256

Power Standards and, 121, 148, 163, 177, 212, 217, 227, 257

as pre- and post-assessments, 125–27

pre-/post-assessment design, 212

times administered, 212, 217

communication. *See also* Problem-Solving Task Write-Up Guide

of mathematical thinking, 29, 30–31, 42

of processes, 33, 35, 63, 195

of understanding, xix, xxi, 67

computational skills, xix, xxii–xxiii, 88. *See also* Step 1: Computational Skills (Math Review and Mental Math)

concepts and, 7

explanation of thinking, 30–31

meaning-based, 3

mental computation. *See* Mental Math

practicing/reviewing, xxiii, xxv, 4, 5, 23

concepts

applying, 30, 31

course-specific, 24

essential, 78, 82, 96–97, 121

focus on, 7

for high-school exit exams, 24

identifying, 13

review of, 4, 5

statistical, 25

understanding of, 47

conceptual understanding, xix–xxiv, 125. *See also* Step 3: Conceptual Understanding

definitions of, 75

developing, 14, 77

need for, 200–201

retaining, 3, 4

Conceptual Understanding Units, xx, 77, 225, 255

aligning with assessments, 126, 216

aligning with Power Standards, 123, 211, 225, 255

aligning with rubrics/scoring guides, 216

bank of, 211, 216, 225, 255

collaboration on, 80, 86, 124–25, 199

collaborative use of, 127

components of, 92

design template, 242–48

designing and using, 78–80, 80–91, 199, 206

duration of, 201

focus of, xxv, 77, 81, 94

grades 7 and 8, 159–62

informal assessment during, 124

in instructional schedule, 182–85

lesson planning and, 79, 86–87, 92

number used per year, 199

pacing schedules/charts and, 202

problem solving and, 30

Problem-Solving Tasks and, 31, 33, 196

reader's assignment, 100

relation of problems to, 4, 211, 215

rubrics for, 79, 85–86, 92

sample, 93–94

sample (grade 6), 143–46

sample (grades 7 and 8), 159–62

sample (high school), 173–76

self-reflection by teacher, 91

confidence, 9, 30, 47, 109

with problem solving, 47, 61

consistency, 131

cooperative groups, 32, 34–35, 48, 51

counting, 101, 147

curriculum design, collaborative, 203

D

data, 136, 138

data analysis, 117, 127, 227, 257

state assessment data, 118

Data Sheets, 34–35

class, 34, 48

directions for, 37–38

independent completion of, 38–39, 48, 53

individual, 52

sample, 42, 43–44, 58

transferring work from, 37–38, 54

Data Teams, 127, 128, 217, 227, 257

decimals, 7, 11

emphasizing, 6

fraction/decimal/percent, 25, 166, 167

grade 6 problems, 136, 137–38

differentiation of instruction, xx, xxvi

assessments for, 85, 117, 212–13, 217, 227, 257

Index

differentiation of instruction
(continued)
  common formative assessment
    for, xx, 121
  mastery of math facts,
    114–15
  Math Review, 21–22, 188
  Math Review Quiz for, 14–16
  problem-solving skills, 49–50
district math programs, xxi–xxii
division, 108
  "think multiplication" strategy,
    138, 147
drawings. *See* graphic
  representation

E

early finishers, 8, 22
eighth grade. *See* grades 7 and 8
encouragement, 8, 56
end-of-unit assessments, 84–85,
    124, 211, 227, 257. *See also*
    post-assessment
  aligning with common
    formative assessments, 124,
    126
  aligning with instruction, xxv
  common formative assessment
    similarity to, 124, 148, 163,
    177
  performance-based, 125, 177
  sample (grade 6), 145
  sample (grades 7 and 8), 161
  sample (high school), 175
English-language learners, 17–18,
    22
enrichment. *See* acceleration
equity, 201
equivalency, 25, 77
error analysis, 189, 190
  in Math Review processing, 9

by teacher, 22
teaching how to do, 10
Essential Questions, xxvi
  for Conceptual Understanding
    Unit topic, 92
  developing, 96
  identifying, 79, 83–84, 126, 216
  as instructional filter, 83,
    86–87
  as instructional guides, 225,
    255
  Math Review Quiz, 14
  Mental Math, 23
  purposes of, 83
  responding to, 85
  sharing with students, 79, 87
  Step 1: Computational Skills
    (Math Review and Mental
    Math), 3
  Step 2: Problem Solving, 29
  Step 3: Conceptual
    Understanding, 75
  Step 4: Mastery of Math Facts,
    101
  Step 5: Common Formative
    Assessment, 117
estimation, 4, 83, 84, 137
evaluation. *See* assessments
explanation of thinking, 30–31,
    50, 194, 195
exponents, 7, 11, 24, 25, 166,
    167–68
  grades 7 and 8 problems, 150,
    151–52

F

fact families, 103, 108
fact retrieval, strategies for,
    102–4, 114, 162, 204, 205
feedback
  from assessments, xxvi, 88, 117

immediate, 16
Math Review Quiz as, 15
professional, 203
to students, 187, 197
timely, 3, 16, 47, 131
via rubric, 70
Five Easy Steps program
  adapting, xxvii
  alignment diagram, 129,
    218–19, 232, 251
  implementation framework,
    220–30, 252–69
  implementing, xix–xx, xxvi,
    130, 182, 207, 209–30
  Step 1. *See* Step 1:
    Computational Skills (Math
    Review and Mental Math)
  Step 2. *See* Step 2: Problem
    Solving
  Step 3. *See* Step 3: Conceptual
    Understanding
  Step 4. *See* Step 4: Mastery of
    Math Facts
  Step 5. *See* Step 5: Common
    Formative Assessment
  time frame/timeline for
    implementation, 217, 221,
    228–30, 258–60, 267–69
  workshop, 211
flex groups, 8, 20, 21, 50
folders
  for math-fact materials, 109
  for student work product, 80,
    90–91
formative assessments, 15,
    20–21, 89, 117. *See also*
    common formative
    assessments
forms. *See* reproducibles
fractions, 24
  denominators, 13, 77
  emphasizing, 6

Index

Index

instruction *(continued)*
    school's current reality, 222,
        252, 261
    teacher-directed, 9–10
    textbooks as guides for,
        198–99
    time for, 119–20, 181–82
    whole-class, 33–34
instructional hours, 119–20
instructional level, 32, 49
instructional sequence, 113–14
    teaching Problem-Solving
        Tasks, 33–39
integers, 166, 167
Internet, 108, 197
interventions, 210, 217, 227, 257
    based on assessment results,
        14, 85, 88
    need for, 20
inverse operations, 103, 147

J

journals, 25, 98
judgment, professional, 202

K

kindergarten math-fact mastery,
    104
knowledge package, 94, 203
knowledge package process, 78,
    94–98
Koopsen, Scott, 18

L

leaders, school. *See* school leaders
leadership teams, 214–17
learning, 200–201
    assessment of. *See* assessments
    emphasis in, 102

expectations, 92, 131
reinforcing, 4
responsibility for, 3, 90
student reflection on, 3, 90
learning objectives, xxi
lesson planning
    backward planning, 124
    for Conceptual Understanding
        Units, 79, 86–87, 92
Lesson Study, 203
literature, 108

M

Ma, Liping, 95
manipulatives, 21, 50, 193
    use with Problem-Solving
        Tasks, 33, 39
Marzano, Robert, 98, 119–20
mastery of math facts, xx. *See
    also* Step 4: Mastery of Math
    Facts
    assessment schedule, 212, 217,
        226, 256
    counting on fingers, 205
    in daily instruction, 206
    differentiation of instruction,
        114–15
    elementary school
        responsibility for, 101, 135,
        149, 165, 212, 226, 256
    grade 6, 147
    at grade levels, 104–5
    grades 7 and 8, 162
    high school, 176
    memorizing facts, 102, 204
    parents and, 105–6, 111, 115,
        206
    patterns for. *See* patterns
    reassessments, 113
    retrieval strategies, 102–4, 114,
        147, 204, 205

    timed work and, 204–5
    timeline for, 101, 104, 106, 115
math facts
    grade-appropriate, 104–5, 116
    groupings, 107
    identifying knowledge of, 114
    mastery of. *See* mastery of
        math facts
    memorization of, 102, 204
    practicing, 106, 107–8, 114,
        147, 162
    state standards re, 104–5, 226,
        256
Math Forum, 32, 56, 141, 155, 171
math problems. *See* problems
math programs, district, xxi–xxii
Math Review, xix, xxv. *See also*
    Step 1: Computational Skills
    (Math Review and Mental
    Math)
    bonus problems, 8, 16, 22, 188
    conceptual unit relation, 6, 88
    daily, 186
    as diagnostic process, 188–89,
        190
    differentiating, 22, 188
    difficulty level and
        progression, 5–6
    executive summary, 210–11
    formats, 215, 223, 253
    frequently asked questions,
        186–206
    grade 6, 135–39
    grades 7 and 8, 149–53
    high school, 165–70
    independent, 135, 149, 165
    key points in processing, 10, 11
    math-fact practice during, 107,
        108–9
    in middle school, 6–7
    new material in, 5, 188
    number of problems, 187

Index

Index

number operations, 24
number properties, 24
number sense, 3, 5
  daily practice with, 23
  development of, xxv, 14, 108–9,
    114, 191, 204–5
  development strategies, 136
  in grade 5, 166
  in grade 6, 136, 137, 147
  in grades 7 and 8, 150, 154, 162
  high school, 170
  math-fact mastery and, 204
  for reasonable answer, 147
  strategies, 9
number system, 204
  patterns in. *See* patterns
  understanding of, 9, 109

O

operations, 24, 103, 108, 162
  fraction, 7
  inverse, 103, 147

P

pacing schedules/charts, 189,
  202–3
parents
  accountability and, 20
  assistance from, 20
  informing of progress, 106, 111,
    113
  math-fact mastery and, 105–6,
    111, 115, 206
  number sense development
    and, 206
  review of student work, 19–20,
    91, 106
part-part-whole relationships, 147
part-whole relationships, 77, 96
"Pass the Pen," 12

patterns
  emphasizing, 114
  knowledge of, 204
  mastery of math facts through,
    102–4, 115, 204, 212, 217,
    226, 256
  Mental Math themes and, 193
  in multiplication, 107–8, 147
  summary, 249–50
  understanding of, xxv
peer assessments, 56, 79, 216,
  224, 254
  post-assessments, 89
  teaching students to do, 72
peers
  assistance from, 5, 8, 18–19, 21,
    188
  guidance from, 5
  interaction with, 47, 50, 61, 195
percent
  emphasizing, 6
  fraction/decimal/percent, 25,
    166, 167
  grades 7 and 8 problems, 150,
    151
  percentage unit, 136, 138
performance. *See also* proficiency
  beginning, 68, 70
  criteria, 63
  exemplary, 68
  levels, 65
  progressing, 68, 70
  reflection on, 15, 17–18, 47
performance assessment. *See*
  assessments
pictures. *See* graphic
  representation
place value, 7, 11
portfolios, 91
post-assessment, 79, 84–85, 89.
  See also common formative
  assessments

aligning with pre-assessment,
  117, 126, 212
common formative assessment
  as, 125, 127
sample, 94
Power Standards, xxv–xxvi,
  119–20
  aligning with Conceptual
    Understanding Units, 123,
    211, 225, 255
  assessment of, 212
  common formative assessment
    and, 121, 148, 163, 177, 212,
    217, 227, 257
  gap analysis, 122–23
  high school, 126
  identifying, 77, 121–23, 126,
    200, 216, 225, 255
  Mental Math themes and, 193
  middle school, 126
  relation of math problems to,
    211
  "unwrapping," 126, 211, 216,
    225, 255
  vertical alignment by grade,
    120–23
practice, 114
  assessments for, 111
  benefits of, 39
  of computational skills, xxiii,
    xxv, 4, 5, 23
  for developing number sense,
    139, 154, 170
  effective, 205
  extra, 113
  feedback and, 3
  materials for, 107–8
  of math facts, 106, 107–8, 114,
    147, 162, 176
  Math Review as, 8
  parental assistance with, 20
  regular, 23, 191, 210

Index

skills, 189, 201

in standards/strands, 4

of strategies, 38, 39, 102, 103

understanding and, 6

pre-assessment, 79, 86, 87

aligning with post-assessment, 117, 126, 212

common formative assessment as, 125

to inform instruction, 124

scoring, 88

Step 4: Mastery of Math Facts, 106–7

Principles and Standards for School Mathematics (NCTM), 29

problem solving. *See also* Step 2: Problem Solving

alternate method steps, 62, 231, 240

assessment of, 216, 224, 254

attitude toward, 51, 53, 61

in balanced math program, xx, xxiii

foundation in, 47

independent, 33, 47, 51, 53

Math Review processing, 9–10

methods, 48, 51–62

multiple approaches to problem, xxi, 4–5, 32, 42, 49, 108

sequence, 47–49

steps, 40–42, 62, 231, 239, 240

strategies, 39, 49, 215, 224, 254

structured activities for, 72

success with, 196

teacher's ability to do, 195–96

teacher's role in, 56, 61

time needed for, 61

value of, 194–95

word problems, 195–96

problems. *See also* Problem-Solving Tasks

bonus. *See* bonus problems

enriching or extending, 32, 41, 49

grade-appropriate, 8

matching to Conceptual Understanding Units, 4, 211, 215

Math Review. *See* Math Review

Mental Math. *See* Mental Math

multiple-step, 38, 211, 215

selecting, 49, 51

in state standardized tests, 6

student needs and, 189–90, 223, 253

teacher's understanding of, 32

word. *See* word problems

problem-solving skills, 49–50

math strategies, 210

promoting, xxi, xxii

Problem-Solving Tasks, 31, 206

bank of, 197

Conceptual Understanding Units and, 31, 33, 196

cooperative group work, 34–35

creating/selecting, 32, 196–97, 224, 254

criteria for good, 31–32

Data Sheets for, 34

difficulty level, 196

elements of, 66–67

independent completion of, 38–39

initial, 63

in instructional schedule, 182–85

instructional sequence for teaching, 33–39

resources for finding/creating, 32

revising work on, 72

rubrics for. *See* rubrics

sample, 42, 42–46

sample (grade 6), 141–42

sample (grades 7 and 8), 156–58

sample (high school), 172–73

selecting, 31–32, 42, 49

teaching students to solve, 33–39

Problem-Solving Task Write-Up, 35

independent completion of, 38–39, 48, 61

sample, 59–60

Problem-Solving Task Write-Up Guide, 35–38, 211

alternate, 51, 52, 53–56, 241

following directions for, 67

frequency of use, 216

in rubric creation, 67

sample, 42, 57–60

template, 73, 211, 236–37

process, 30–31, 66, 67

professional development, xx–xxi, 215, 216

proficiency, 63, 70

criteria for, 67–68, 131

demonstrating, 16, 71, 72, 113

programs, commercial, 189–90

proof, 67, 195

Q

quality, 89–90

R

ratio/proportion, 166, 168

reasonable answer, 4, 6, 210

emphasizing, 9, 11, 108, 215, 223, 253

in Math Review processing, 137–38

Index

Index

Index

V

Van De Walle, John, 75, 102–3, 104

verification, 42, 55–56, 67, 195

vocabulary, 210, 215
  assessment results and, 98–99
  English-language learners and, 22, 49
  in Math Review processing, 13
  in Mental Math, 24, 26–27
  posting, 30, 49
  in rubrics, 63–65
  in Step 1, 223, 253
  in Step 3, 225, 255

teaching, 98–99
transition words, 38, 41
use of, 29, 41, 67

W

whole-class instruction, 33–34

word problems, 195–96. *See also* problems; Problem-Solving Tasks
  bonus problems in Math Review, 8
  strategies for solving, 39

worksheets, 108

writing. *See also* Problem-Solving Task Write-Up

communicating understanding in, xxi
on Data Sheets, 53
description of process, 211
explanation of thinking, 194
formats for. *See* Problem-Solving Task Write-Up Guide
including in math program, 29–30, 108
math vocabulary in, 13
modeling, 50
as problem-solving step, 41
self-reflection and, 17–18, 79, 90
sharing, 30
transition words, 38, 41

Power Standards
Identifying the Standards That Matter the Most

Larry Ainsworth

Power Standards presents a proven process for identifying the standards that matter the most, a process that can be used successfully with every state's standards in every content area and at every grade level. The book is designed to be a step-by-step, practical manual that educators can use immediately in their own districts to replicate the process others have successfully followed.

In all fifty states, standards have become the critical focus for achieving the results that schools are expected to produce. However, educators know that most states have too many standards to be taught effectively during one academic year. Striving to cover everything, educators admit to teaching many of the standards only superficially. In addition, educators often consider all standards equal when, in fact, *certain standards are more important than others.*

Now, in **Power Standards,** Larry Ainsworth shows all educators not only how to create a prioritized subset of their own state or district standards, but also how to use these Power Standards to guide the development of meaningful curriculum and assessment. The straightforward and easy-to-read format enables readers to immediately apply these proven, practical strategies. Now, educators can significantly improve achievement for all students— by first identifying the standards that matter the most!

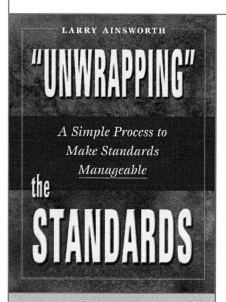

"Unwrapping" the Standards
A Simple Process to Make Standards <u>Manageable</u>

Larry Ainsworth

"Unwrapping" the standards is a technique to provide educators with a proven process to identify in the wording of the standards what students must know and be able to do. The result is more effective instructional planning and assessment that result in increased student learning. From the "unwrapped" concepts and skills, educators next determine the Big Ideas (end learning goals) that they want their students to remember long after instruction ends, and then write Essential Questions to guide students toward understanding of these Big Ideas. In these pages, readers will find practical tools:

- **Step-by-step instructions to complete the process**

- **More than 85 examples of "unwrapped" standards for grades K–12 in numerous content areas**

In ***"Unwrapping" the Standards,*** Larry Ainsworth shares his experience in use of the "unwrapping" process with K–12 educators across the country. He explains how to identify the Big Ideas—what educators want their students to remember long after instruction ends—and how to formulate Essential Questions to focus instruction and assessment. The final goal of "unwrapping" is for students to learn each of the "unwrapped" concepts and skills and to be able to respond to the Essential Questions with Big Ideas stated in their own words.

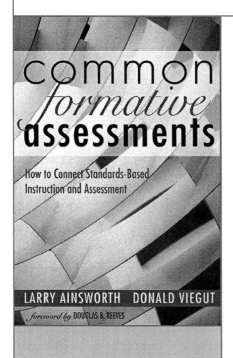

Common Formative Assessments
How to Connect Standards-Based Instruction and Assessment

Larry Ainsworth and Donald Viegut

Now you have powerful means to closely align curriculum, instruction, and assessment to the standards essential for student success. You will learn how teams of teachers in the same content area or grade level can collaboratively develop, test, and refine common formative assessments in order to gain reliable and timely feedback on student progress. The results provide teachers with critical insight into how well students are understanding the standards, what changes are needed in instructional strategies, and how to best meet the needs of every student!

This timely resource presents the "big picture" of an integrated standards-based instruction and assessment system, and offers instructional leaders and teacher teams guidelines for:

- **Developing high-quality common formative assessments.**

- **Aligning school-based common formative assessments with district benchmarks and large-scale summative assessments.**

- **Predicting likely student performance on subsequent assessments in time to make instructional modifications.**

- **Implementing and sustaining common formative assessments within the school's or district's assessment culture.**

This book is a must-read for all educators and leaders committed to improving standards-based assessment practices in their district, school, or classroom.

Write to Know Series from Advanced Learning Press

Nonfiction Writing Prompts for Math
Middle School

Jan Christinson

One of the most powerful practices any teacher of K–12 mathematics can do is to teach students the importance of being able to communicate, verbally and in writing, the process they used to solve multiple-step problems.

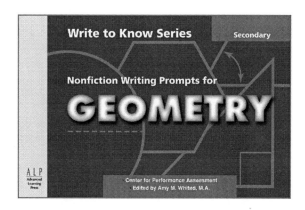

Nonfiction Writing Prompts for Geometry
Secondary

Center for Performance Assessment

Writing in mathematics provides an open forum for student and teacher to engage in thoughtful conversations about the mathematics they are learning. . . . It really allows the teacher to ascertain what's happening between the student's "ears."

Nonfiction Writing Prompts for Algebra
Secondary

Center for Performance Assessment

When students write about their understanding of math processes, the teacher can assess their true knowledge.

What Educators and Leaders
Are Saying about *Five Easy Steps*

We are using this framework extensively in our school district. Five Easy Steps to a Balanced Math Program *helps teachers focus on teaching concepts for understanding, as opposed to marching through a textbook. We emphasize that our state standards are our curriculum, and this is the framework we are using to plan and teach these standards for understanding to our students. Textbooks, like any other resource, are incidental to the implementation of quality math teaching and learning. We are working toward conceptual understanding and not just teaching the procedures of math the same way we were all taught math. Our teachers are excited about Math Review and Mental Math. Our students are excited about the Problem of the Week. We are all excited about math in our district and the results we are getting with our students.*

> Virginia P. Foley, Ed.D.
> Director of Elementary Curriculum
> and Student Services
> Dalton Public Schools

Five Easy Steps to a Balanced Math Program *has revolutionized the way our teachers approach math instruction! The five steps not only represent best practice, they are easy to understand and can be implemented by our teachers immediately following awareness/training sessions. The philosophy of the five steps reinforces our desire to create mathematically powerful students.* Five Easy Steps to a Balanced Math Program *is so highly regarded in our school district, it has made our list of "non-negotiable" professional practices!*

> **Michele Walker**
> Mathematics/Science/Assessment
> Coordinator
> Metropolitan School District
> of Wayne Township
> Indianapolis, IN
> Dalton, GA

Five Easy Steps to a
Balanced Math Program
for Secondary Grades